HEALER WITHIN

THE HEALER WITHIN

How to Awaken and Develop your Healing Potential

DAVID FURLONG

Acknowledgements

I wish to express my sincere appreciation for all the help and support that I have had in writing this book, in particular the following individuals who read the text and gave valuable feedback and advice: Nancy Allen, Claire Furlong, Linda Jenkins, 'Paddy' Clarke, Nerys Dee, Marjatta Pappadakis and Dr Linda Powell. I also wish to thank all my colleagues and students for their insights and shared experiences that have helped build the fund of knowledge that is found within these pages

I would also like to thank my editors Gill Cormode and Anne Lawrance for their patience and guidance in getting this book to completion.

The extracts from the Tao are taken from *The Tao of Peace* by Diane Dreher (Donald I. Fine, Inc, New York/Mandala, London, 1991).

Originally published in 1995 as *The Complete Healer* by
Judy Piatkus (Publishers) Ltd
5 Windmill Street, London W1P 1HF
www.piatkus.co.uk

This edition published in 1998
Reprinted 1999 (three times)

A catalogue record for this book is available from the British Library

ISBN 0-7499-1877-2

Edited by Carol Franklin
Designed by Sue Ryall

Set in Imprint by Computerset, Harmondsworth
Printed and bound in Great Britain by
Butler & Tanner Ltd, Frome and London

Contents

To HA
for his great inspiration

Foreword

Healing has been practised in every known culture throughout recorded history. Western science has been sceptical of healing, believing it to be no more than the effects of suggestion, wishful thinking, denial of illness, avoidance of facing our human mortality, or even a fraud.

Surprisingly, there has been more scientific research on healing than on most of the other complementary therapies. Out of 155 controlled studies reviewed in my book, *Healing Research, volume 1,* more than half show significant effects. There can be no doubt that these do not represent suggestion or placebo effects, because in addition to studies on humans there are many studies on animals, plants, bacteria, yeasts, cells in laboratory culture, enzymes and more.

Despite the available evidence, conventional medicine remains sceptical. I hasten to add that I am not writing this to condemn allopathic doctors and nurses. Their training and professional associations have taught them to be cautious about accepting new treatments. There is always the possibility that a treatment might be harmful because it is toxic or ineffectual.

My own training as a medical doctor in America, with experience in research and specialisation in psychiatric psychotherapy, led me to be as cautious and sceptical as the rest of my colleagues. Though fifteen years ago I was interested in complementary therapies, I was of the firm opinion that healing could be no more than suggestion, self delusion or the work of charlatans. I had heard of the miraculous cures of healers but believed that these must surely be wild exaggerations or changes brought about in people who had illnesses which would have got better anyway. It was not until I observed a healer bringing about a physical change in half an hour through a laying-on of hands that I was willing to begin to consider that healing might be a real and potent therapy. It was not a major change, but it was a significant one. A young man, about 20 years old, had a lump growing under his nipple. It hurt when he engaged in college wrestling, and he was scheduled for a surgical removal of the lump. Though he did not believe in healing, he was willing to give it a chance in order to avoid surgery.

I felt the lump with my fingers, noting that it measured one by two centimetres, was rubbery firm (like a rubber on a pencil), more fixed than one would like to see in a lesion of this sort (suggesting it might be a cancer growing into the surrounding tissues), and quite tender. Fortunately there was another doctor observing the healing with me. Together we measured the lesion before and after the healing, agreeing on its size and consistency. After the healing, the lump had shrunk by a centimetre, was soft, freely mobile, and non-tender. Without having a medical colleague to confirm my measurements, I am sure I would have convinced myself that I had either mismeasured the lesion or misremembered the measurements. Such a change simply does not occur in half an hour in such a lump.

My next step after that was to go to the research literature, which is a doctor's way of reassuring himself that a treatment is valid. Satisfied that others had found demonstrable effects with healing, I continued to study *about* healing over several years. This included talking with healers, setting up a research study myself, and reading omnivorously about healers and related subjects.

It was only two years later that I dared to take the step of studying the doing of healing myself. I had to overcome my misconceptions that if I developed my own healing gifts I would be unscientific, or biased in such a way that I could not 'impartially' observe and consider what healing was or wasn't. I realised that there is really no such thing as being neutral to healing. There is simply a spectrum of beliefs about healing, and one is somewhere along the spectrum between disbelief and belief.

It is good to find that the climate of attitudes towards healing is shifting towards much greater acceptance amongst the public in general and the medical community in particular. The UK is a world leader in the integration of healing with conventional medical practice. Healers such as David Furlong are now treating patients referred by doctors. Some healers have been invited to work in GP surgeries. They also work in hospital pain, cancer, cardiac rehabilitation and arthritis centres. Some of the healers are paid under the NHS. The Doctor-Healer Network which I founded in 1988 invites doctors, nurses and other conventional carers to meet regularly with healers and other complementary therapists to explore how patients may benefit from the broadest spectrum of approaches. Some of the doctors are now exploring the development of their own healing gifts. I have been able to arrange Postgraduate Education Allowance approved courses in stress management for doctors which include the study of healing.

In view of the fact that so many people are realising the importance and potential of healing, it is good to find David's book explaining healing in easily accessible terms and introducing a spectrum of exercises which can help readers to explore and develop their own gifts. I have known David for several years, and have been impressed with his commitment to studying and teaching healing.

Being the complex creatures we are, each of us is unique in our makeup. David wisely suggests a range of approaches through which we may come to understand and heal ourselves and others. No single approach is adequate for everyone, or perhaps even for any single person. Furthermore, what may help to bring about understanding and healing in a given person today, may be inadequate or inappropriate for another situation tomorrow. Having a spectrum of approaches makes it possible to deal with a broad range of situations.

David points out that healing starts with self healing of the healer. This is a most important observation. We are far better at offering healing to others when we have the experience of undergoing healing ourselves. This also serves as a reminder to us, as healers, that people have the capacity and responsibility to contribute to their own healings.

One ought to have a map if one is to explore new territory. David provides a number of ways in which we can understand healing. Healing may involve subtle energies which are readily perceptible if we but open ourselves to them. These energies may be focused by one's mind and David suggests ways in which one may exercise and focus the mind through meditations and visualisations, so that one's abilities to use these energies may be enhanced.

This book also delineates several levels at which healing may occur. To some it may appear confusing that there isn't a single, clear explanation for healing. This is a true reflection of the human condition. Words and simple theories are inadequate to dissect and describe the complexities of creatures comprised of body, emotions, mind, relationships and spirit.

The reader is warmly recommended to this book for a start along the path of healing. This path may lead to a lifetime of inner awarenesses and personal growth.

Dr Daniel Benor
February 1995

Introduction

'You have healing hands', or something similar, is a remark that has propelled more individuals into starting healing than any other single comment. Certainly, it is the main reason that people give me for attending one of my introductory healing courses. The exciting thing, from my perception, is that most individuals possess a healing potential, which like any skill can be readily developed to the benefit of everyone. All that is required is a little patience, application and a desire to help others. *The Complete Healer* will show you, in a clear, step-by-step way, how to awaken and give expression to your 'healing energy (Ch'i)'. You will discover effective ways to balance your own energies as well as directing healing to others.

In a recent article in the *Nursing Times* Dr Daniel Benor asserted that 90 per cent of all doctors and nurses who attended his healing courses displayed a measure of healing ability. Many therapists and members of the health service have discovered the great value of healing within their respective disciplines. But this does not mean to say that you have to be a member of the medical profession to develop your healing skills; far from it. Healers in Britain come from all walks of life and professions. They apply their gift to helping friends, colleagues, members of their family and pets, as well as to those who might be referred on to them for specialist treatment.

Whatever your occupation or lifestyle, understanding and utilising the principles and techniques contained herein will enrich your life.

For those who are already practising healers this book contains many practical exercises and techniques that will further expand your knowledge of this field. It is based on my life's exposure to healing and the many training courses that I have run over the past 26 years, helping people to discover and awaken this natural talent. In my healing work I have met a wide array of different types of cases, from simple problems like cuts and burns to complex situations involving family karma or ancestral patterns. It has taken me into treating mental illness as well as balancing the energy of places, which often necessitates the release of spirits or souls that have become stuck out of time. On a daily level it is a skill that I use to help maintain the health and well-being of my children and other members of my family. In practice its applications are limitless and I continually feel a deep sense of privilege whenever I have the opportunity to express this gift.

The healing techniques given here are based on four simple concepts:

- that we are composed of energy (Ch'i) on many levels, that links the physical body to the spiritual self;
- all dis-ease stems from imbalances within this spectrum of energy and all imbalances can be corrected by right action;
- when two or more people, or living things, come together subtle energy is exchanged between them that can be either beneficial or disharmonious according to the circumstances;
- that there are sources of energy outside of ourselves that can be drawn upon to improve our health, vitality and well-being.

By understanding how energy flows within the various aspects of your being, you can help maintain inner balance and, in so doing, considerably improve your health and vitality. In a similar way *The Complete Healer* will show you how to balance the dynamic within relationships, so benefiting all your dealings with other people whether they be at work, in leisure or at home. These principles will further be expanded to explain how to direct energy to bring healing to your friends, members of the family and others. As part of this process you will discover ways to tap sources of external energy that can nourish and sustain all your endeavours. This is not difficult, nor is the ability to heal an unachievable goal, but it is readily available to you now. By awakening and developing your healing potential you will find a sense of purpose and well-being that will touch all aspects of your life.

The power to heal is not a vague notion, but is now gaining increasing scientific validation, based upon many rigorous trials. In 1987 a remarkable medical study was carried out by Dr Randolph Byrd, in the USA, to assess the effectiveness or otherwise of the power of distant healing. Over a 10-month period around 400 patients who had been admitted to the coronary care unit of the San Francisco General Hospital took part in a clinical trial in which half the group received healing 'prayer' treatment, alongside their normal medical care. It was a double blind test, designed according to rigid criteria, with neither the patients, doctors nor nurses being aware that they were part of a medical study. The results, when they came back, showing the beneficial effects of healing, were so significant that had a drug or clinical procedure been involved it would certainly have been heralded as a major breakthrough.

The procedures adopted in this study are very revealing for they reinforce ideas held by many healers based on their own empirical experience. It has long been recognised that healing is effective over a distance and by some amazing inner knowing the healing energy connects to the person it is being directed at, even if the healer has never met that individual and has had only the briefest of descriptions. In the Byrd study just the person's first name was given to the prayer groups.

Over the last ten years many similar scientific studies have been carried out, based on healers directing energy to sick people as well as to animals, plants and cell cultures. Mounting evidence supports the notion that the vast majority of us possess this 'gift of healing' and that it can be advantageously developed to help both ourselves and others.

The Complete Healer will also show you how to deal with two problems that affect most people at some stage in their life. These are:

- being disturbed by the energy of others;
- being drained of energy.

Many sensitive individuals today feel battered by the energies of people or buildings that they find disturbing. In certain cases this can become so overwhelming that some individuals find it impossible to go into supermarkets or other crowded places. Lacking vitality, or feeling exhausted for no obvious cause, is also a very common problem. This is especially the case among some groups, like teachers and healthcare workers. There are simple techniques explained in this book that will show you how to overcome these two debilitating handicaps, so freeing you to lead a healthy, productive life.

As part of healing development, you will discover how to access your inner wisdom and harness the power of your 'psychic senses'. These are seen as aspects of your spiritual self that can be called upon whenever you need to make clear decisions or find direction in your life. The skills learned can be directed to gaining insight into general problems, and the causes of energy imbalances both in yourself and others.

The Complete Healer draws from the wisdom of Chinese belief as well as many other traditions. The techniques described here can be used readily by anyone interested in awakening their healing gifts. All the exercises can be worked safely at home, except where specifically mentioned, providing you with many opportunities to develop your amazing inner potential. As with all things in life practice makes perfect. By just spending a few minutes each day you can awaken so much untapped richness. This book will help you unlock the enormous power that is waiting to be discovered within. It lies in your capability to express your healing potential, to find health, vitality, joy, creativity and wholeness.

CHAPTER 1

The Tao Of Healing

The Tao is the One,
From the One come yin and yang,
From these two, creative Ch'i;
From Ch'i, ten thousand things,
The forms of all creation.

(TAO 42)

The word Tao (pronounced 'dao') comes from Ancient China. It means the 'Way of right action' and stems from a work called the *Tao Te Ching*, reputedly written by the legendary Lao Tzu in the sixth century BC. The *Tao Te Ching* with the *I Ching* and the commentaries of Confucius, laid the foundations for the great wisdom that has come out of China in understanding the causes of illness and unhappiness. It gives direction on what we need to do to correct imbalances within us to maintain health and harmony. When we follow the Tao we discover our source of happiness, inner peace and well-being.

The Tao is based on a flow of energy known as Ch'i, which is expressed in two forms called yin and yang. Every aspect of creation was seen as a weaving together of these two aspects of Ch'i. Yin energy is passive, receptive and yielding. In electrical terms it is the negative pole of battery. Yang energy is active, outgoing and firm; it is the positive pole of the battery.

Health is dependent upon balancing Ch'i within us

and, as an example, the development of acupuncture is based on this principle. But Ch'i can be balanced in many ways and it operates over many spectrums. In simple terms we could say that there is the Ch'i of the body, the Ch'i of the emotions, the Ch'i of the mind and the Ch'i of the soul or spirit. Each level needs to be balanced both within itself and between each layer for health to exist. In this book you will discover how you can use your mind and thoughts to channel Ch'i to correct imbalances on every level of your being.

This energy can also be used to benefit others. As the Tao says:

> *The Tao person aids others*
> *So no one is lost,*
> *And uses things wisely,*
> *So nothing is wasted.*
>
> (TAO 27)

By helping others we help ourselves and when we help ourselves we help others; life is always a two-way flow. Exercises in this book will focus both on teaching you how to direct energy to others to aid their healing process and how to balance your own energies for self-healing.

The Power to Heal

To understand how and why healing works we need to consider the concept of energy or Ch'i in greater detail. The dictionary defines energy as '*the ability or capacity to produce an effect and science further restricts it to being a product of the physical world*'. The healing activity, demonstrated in Randolph Byrd's experiment (see the Introduction) and other similar studies cannot be understood in terms of known physical laws, yet all the evidence suggests that directed prayer or healing thoughts produce an effect. This certainly falls within the wider definition of energy. To understand how this works we need to assume the existence of other frequencies of energy that lie beyond the range of known force–energies that can be controlled or influenced directly by our thinking processes.

Professor Rhine in the USA over many years carried out repeated experiments into telepathy. Statistical evidence shows that many people have this ability and I am sure that at some stage of your life you have experienced uncanny cases of seeming telepathic communication, those incidents when, for no apparent reason, you start to think of someone only to find a few minutes later that they are on the phone or you bump into them in the street. In my case the more I believed that this was possible the more often it occurred until now it happens quite regularly.

More dramatic still are the highly impressive studies that have been carried out by Professor Robert Jahn of Princeton University. Using electronic random generators he has demonstrated that by simply thinking into the apparatus the mind is able to influence the randomness of these machines. The subjects who have taken part in these studies have been ordinary people, showing that this power is available to most of us. In the original studies the individuals sat in close proximity to the machine, but subsequently Professor Jahn has demonstrated the same effect when the tester is several miles from the equipment. Many scientists have dismissed Professor Jahn's findings because they defy the known laws of physics, but this bi-location effect is well known within healing circles. Indeed, it was demonstrated in the studies of Dr Byrd.

This raises an important fundamental point to do with our beliefs. Ample scientific research has demonstrated a strange force known as the 'experimenter effect'. This means that the concepts and attitudes of the experimenter profoundly affect the experiment. If you strongly believe something to be true, or not true, you increase considerably the likelihood that your experiments will validate your original idea. If we believe something to be true then it enhances the potential for it to be so. The prayer group participants believed that their prayers would be effective. The belief that I am telepathic increases considerably my potential to pick up another's thoughts, particularly when the logical side of my mind does not actively interfere.

EXERCISE

Exploring Telepathy

Try it for yourself. Sit quietly for a moment and affirm to yourself 'I have a telepathic ability'. Really believe the truth of this statement and see what happens over the next few days. The trick is not to try to pick up another's thoughts: just observe those moments when you start to think of someone. You can then check it back by asking them what they were doing or thinking of at the same time. This will demonstrate clearly that belief is a very important ingredient in the healing process.

Resonance and the Tuning Fork Effect

The way that Ch'i is interchanged can best be understood in terms of resonance. Professor Alan Wolf explains this process by saying, '*The fundamental proposition is that everything is vibrating, everything is vibration. If you can vibrate with it, or attune to whatever it is that is vibrating a resonance is created; then you have a way of transferring energy back and forth'*. Put simply, if two people in the same room each hold a tuning fork pitched to the same note and one tuning fork is sounded, the other will start to vibrate as well, as the resonant energy is transferred between the two. At a mental level if you set up a connecting resonance with someone else, and generally this is done by just thinking of them, then energy can be transferred back and forth. This energy or Ch'i can be used for healing or telepathic communication.

Are You a Radio Station?

Perhaps the easiest way of looking at it is to see yourself as a radio station both broadcasting and receiving information all the time. The bulk of this inputting information you will screen out, but just occasionally

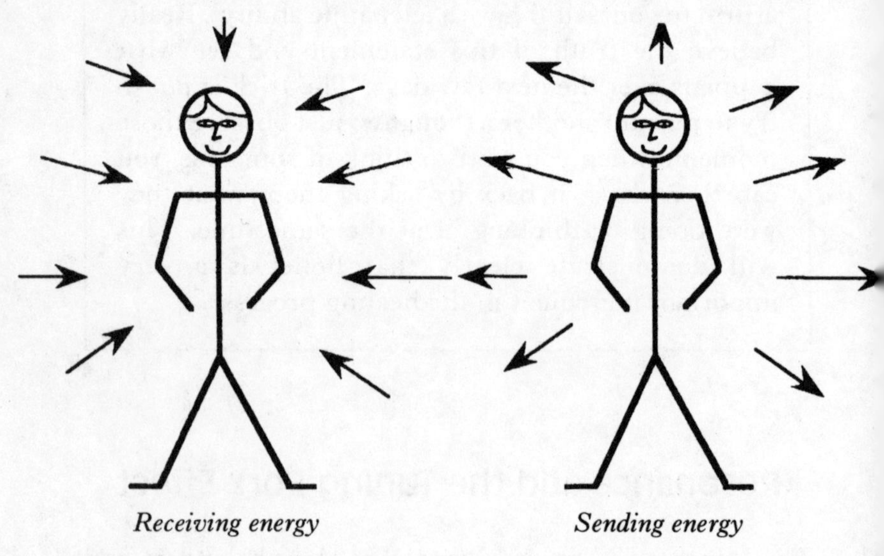
Receiving energy *Sending energy*

some of it seeps through. The more you develop your sensitivity to this incoming data the more you can start to pick it up. This can give you enormous insights into all sorts of situations and may also warn you when something is amiss with others. There have been cases where people's lives have been saved by the prompt intervention of someone else, warned of an emergency only by a sudden feeling or intuition that something was wrong. In essence, all that is required to develop this type of sensitivity is to just 'listen' to what your feelings, perceptions and hunches are telling you and not dismiss them out of hand. There is a tendency to disregard what cannot be logically proved which is why so much input gets filtered out.

However, this level of awareness, if not handled correctly, can have its own problems. Sensitive people can find that they become very upset by chaotic energies that they sense around themselves, such as can be found in crowded places. Its rather like trying to listen to 101 radio stations all broadcasting at the same time. Such people can also be seriously affected when others get angry or display aggressive emotions towards them. So there are valid reasons why we naturally block out much of this informational energy. The more receptive we become the more we need tools to deal effectively with its attendant problems. On the other side of the coin we can learn to project our thoughts to others to help balance their energies. Dealing effectively with these problems will be discussed more fully in Chapter 5 of this book.

Science tells us that energy flows from the stronger to the weaker force; in electrical terms from the positive pole to the negative. It is a similar process in human exchange. Many of you will have experienced the phenomenon of just sitting with someone, an elderly person perhaps, and very quickly feeling totally exhausted. It is as though all the energy has drained out of you. By connecting with this person, just sitting in their company, resonances are set up that allow energy to flow. If their Ch'i is depleted you will feel energy being drained out of you as the energy seeks a point of equilibrium. Conversely, you will also be able to think of

Energy Imbalance

The two energy fields will seek a point of equilibrium with Ch'i draining from the woman to the man. This will cause the man to feel more enlivened while the woman will suddenly become tired.

those occasions when a dynamic or inspiring individual has filled you with the enthusiasm or additional drive to complete a task. This is the same process as before but in reverse. Understanding how you can manipulate and balance your energy reservoirs is one of the important keys to healing, both for yourself and others.

Energy Flow and Resonance in Complementary Therapies

The majority of therapies in the complementary field are based on this principle of energy flow and resonance. Homoeopathic remedies, for example, are produced by taking a substance, diluting it in an alcohol/water solution and shaking it vigorously. The resulting mixture is then further diluted and shaken on a 100:1 basis, with the one part being the mixture. This process is repeated a number of times until, in the majority of preparations,

Healthy energy exchange

there are no molecules of the original substance left. Yet these are some of the most potent homoeopathic remedies. Effectively the water has taken on the memory or vibration of the original substance and it is this which acts on the corresponding resonances within the body, resulting hopefully in a cure. Apart from healing some of the other therapies that work directly on balancing the subtle energy fields of our being include acupuncture, radionics, reflexology, shiatsu and cranial osteopathy. Healing, as we shall see, can involve:

- the introduction of energy into the system;
- balancing what is already there; or
- in some cases removing energies that are not appropriate.

Your Self-Healing Mechanisms

We all possess very powerful self-healing mechanisms that correct imbalances as soon as they occur, except in disease situations. Cut yourself and the repair mechanisms of your body immediately respond. If you are infected by a virus the white blood cells of your immune system will come to your assistance. The body continually seeks homoeostasis or general equilibrium and we become ill when this balance is disturbed to any large extent. Learning how to balance your Ch'i will go a long way to preventing imbalances occurring in the first place. Exercises on Ch'i balancing techniques are given in Chapter 3. Sometimes, for many different reasons, dis-ease can occur. You will find techniques throughout this book to highlight where the imbalances lie and, more importantly, what can be done to restore harmony.

The self-healing process occurs at a level below normal conscious thought. You do not have to tell your white blood cells to attack a foreign body, they do this automatically. Sending out healing thoughts to another individual works in a similar way. An innate knowing at a deep level of consciousness will draw forth the right energy pattern to correct the imbalance. Put another way, your body knows how to correct most imbalances when they occur, given the right circumstances. When it comes to helping another you can learn to tap into this 'inner knowing' and project the correct balancing resonances or energy to help the individual regain balance for themselves. In practice we never 'heal' anyone; all we can do is help another heal themselves.

Many new healers become anxious about whether they are sending the healing correctly. It is important to learn to trust your own 'inner knowing' and not worry about whether you are doing the right thing. The most important quality in any interchange of Ch'i is intention. If your intention is to send healing, balancing thoughts to another then what is right for them will emerge. So there is no one to heal, for we are all unique and have our own natural balance or matrix of energy. Because of this, when you give healing, you will be better suited to helping some cases or conditions than others. You need not worry at this stage about this, for experience will soon indicate where your natural strengths lie. As a healer you will need to discover the method that suits you best and in practice the only 'correct' system of healing is the one that works for the individual healer.

Projecting Healing Ch'i

Projecting healing energy, either to yourself or others, is controlled by conscious thought. In this, intention and visualisation (or imaging) are the two most important constituents. Visualisation is the ability to hold a picture image in the mind that corresponds to the idea being thought about. It does not have to be exact in every detail but should at least approximate to what is being considered. For example, if I asked you to describe your front door you would need to call upon your visual memory to do this. Some people would 'see' the image of the door very clearly in their mind, others might just have a vague sense of what it looked like. But in both cases some form of imaging would have to occur to describe the door. Some individuals find visualisation difficult. Alternatives are suggested in Chapter 3, but visual images form a powerful link with the deeper layers of our consciousness and have traditionally been used as part of the healing process.

Remember that all healing should be an offering, like leading a horse to water. You cannot try to force the horse to drink, nor should you try. We each have our own path to tread, and for some this may mean experiencing disease and suffering. Such individuals will in consequence reject those aspects of healing that seek to remove the symptoms. In practice few people reject healing completely, as long as it is given in the right spirit.

Limitless Ch'i

One of the problems that healers often experience when they are beginners is feeling depleted of Ch'i themselves

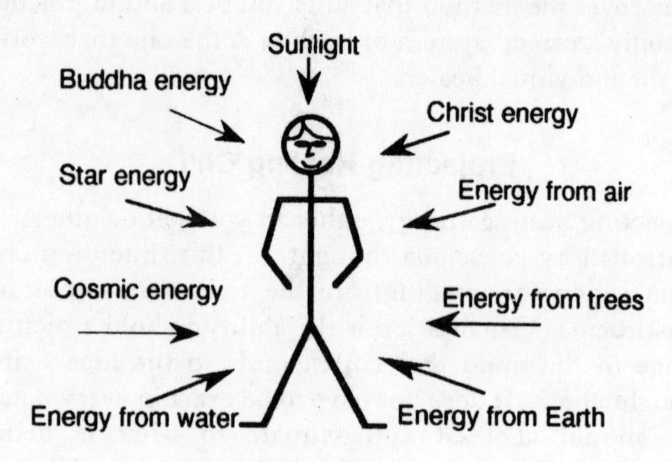

Sources of Ch'i

after they have given healing. If we go back to the image of each of us holding our own reservoir of energy, you will see that passing some of your energy on to another will soon run you dry. The solution is to learn to connect to sources of energy or Ch'i outside of yourself; of which there are a vast array in the universe. For example, a Christian might see Christ as a source of Ch'i, while a Shaman might link to the earth, and each would be successful. Learning to channel Ch'i considerably expands your natural range of frequencies and allows a more potent form of energy to flow through you. Indeed this is one of the most important principles in life. In discussing this topic with a well-known concert musician, Nicholas Daniel, he happened to remark that it was only when he looked to drawing on an energy outside of himself that his performances really took off. When previously he relied just on his own energy, his own Ch'i, he would end the performance feeling totally drained of energy. Yet once he had learned to connect to this external source he would finish the concert feeling as invigorated as when he began.

It does not matter what your profession or task in life is. There will be very few individuals who do not at some stage require extra Ch'i. There is an abundant supply within the universe, and all you need to do is reach out and grasp it.

The Ch'i of Love

One of the most powerful healing energies that we can draw upon is the Ch'i of love. You could see this as the 'love' of God, Allah, Jehovah, or symbolically as the goddess Aphrodite or Isis. It does not really matter.

'Love' energy may be said to carry three primary qualities. It protects, transforms and harmonises, which is why it is so helpful in the healing process. We will discuss some other potential sources of energy in Chapter 5 when we look at healing techniques. However establishing the principle is important at this stage.

As the Tao states:

The people of Tao transcend self
Through loving compassion
Find themselves
In a higher sense.
Through loving service
They attain fulfilment.

(TAO 7)

EXERCISE

Projecting Healing Ch'i to Another Person

(fifteen minutes)

The following exercise will show you how healing Ch'i can be projected to another person and will show you how to work with the creativity of your mind through visual images.

Sit comfortably in an upright chair or cross-legged on a cushion if you prefer. Your back should be straight. Close your eyes and for a few moments focus on your breathing. Feel that it is gentle and relaxed. Next think of the quality of 'love'. What does it mean to you? Visualise an answer to the following questions:

- Which colour do I associate with 'love'?
- Where would I locate this quality within my body?
- What animal do I associate with 'love' and where is that animal standing in relation to me?
- What flower do I associate with 'love'?
- What item of clothing do I associate with 'love' and what do I feel when I wear this in my imagination?
- Now think of a person who is very dear to me and project a thought of love towards them.
- Next think of someone who needs help and send them a thought of love.
- Now think of someone with whom you don't get on and send them a thought of love.
- Finally, send yourself a thought of love, thinking particularly of those aspects that you dislike about yourself.

When you have finished bring yourself back to waking consciousness and open your eyes.

You might find it useful to write down what you experienced, how you felt emotionally and what symbolic images came up. The important thing with symbols is **not** to reject what comes forward. Beginners will often say, 'I didn't like that animal, so I changed it for another'. The deepest part of your being will communicate important messages through symbols to your conscious mind, so it can become an enormously rich source of inner wisdom and knowing. Learn to interpret the symbols, not reject them.

Summary

- Energy is the ability or capacity to produce an effect.
- To comprehend how healing works we need to accept that there are frequencies of energy or Ch'i beyond the physical realm.
- Energies flow when two things resonate together.
- Energies flow from the stronger force to the weaker.
- Just thinking of someone opens up the potential for Ch'i to be exchanged.
- Intention in healing is all important.
- In order not to deplete yourself energetically when healing you need to learn to connect to sources of energy or Ch'i outside of yourself.
- Love is a powerful healing energy that harmonises, transforms and protects.

CHAPTER 2

The Nature Of Your Being

The Tao gives birth to one,
One gives birth to two,
Two gives birth to three
Three gives birth to all things.

(TAO 42)

How Ch'i Operates

Having explored how energy or Ch'i connects between individuals we now need to consider how it operates within us. This is particularly important in helping you understand the causes of ill-health and the steps you can take to maintain balance within.

The most dense level of your energy field is the physical body. Science tells us that this is composed of atoms and molecules held together in a particular matrix or form that you recognise as yourself. Predominantly you are space, with the individual atoms acting as focal points of energy. The atomic structure holds phenomenal power which is evidenced when atoms are split in nuclear reactions. It is interesting to reflect on the vast potential energy that we hold within us. We are all aware of our physical self, particularly when something is out of balance or in a state of dis-ease, but it also provides us

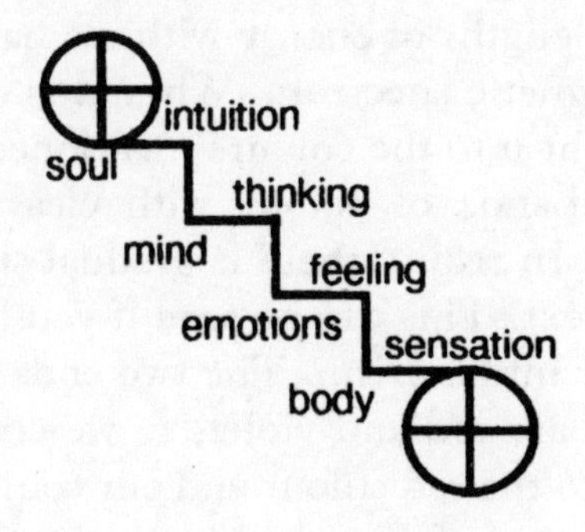

Step down of energy

with many wonderful rich experiences.

The physical body forms one end of the spectrum of your energies, while the other end is the part of you that is generally referred to as the soul, spiritual self, or higher self. You could equally call it your 'core essence', 'divine spark' or whatever name you choose to represent the inner motivating energy that gives you life. Religious belief affirms that without the energy of our soul the body ceases to function and death ensues. Within this aspect could be seen to reside your inner wisdom and higher consciousness or the part of you that can provide insight, direction and illumination to your life, if you can but access it.

We can measure the energy frequencies of the physical body with scientific instruments but we cannot measure directly the Ch'i of the spiritual self because it is vibrating at a much finer level. We can, however, understand the principles that link these two parts of ourselves by using some simple analogies.

The Rainbow Bridge

The first example we could consider is the visible light spectrum made up of the colours red, orange, yellow, green, blue, indigo and violet. Light is formed by vibrating wavelengths of energy within a narrow band of the electro-magnetic spectrum. While it is convenient to classify this light into the colours mentioned above, they are not fixed bands of colour with clear delineations between them. In reality there is gradual shift from one colour to the next. This can be seen if you look carefully at a rainbow or into a prism. The two ends of the visible light spectrum are red and violet, so we could liken our physical body to the red colour and our soul to the violet. Every other aspect of ourselves, our emotions, feelings, thoughts, imagination, ego, subconscious self and whatever other part we can conceive of, falls between these two poles like the other colours of the rainbow; each merging gradually from one state to the next.

The Symphony of the Self

Another analogy we could use is liken ourselves to a piano, where the base notes represent the physical body and the top notes the spiritual self. Western music is based on a scale of notes called an octave, represented by the letters 'A' to 'G'. These notes form a resonating group that is mirrored by corresponding octaves at a higher and lower pitch. In a grand piano there are seven octaves so, to be more specific, we could liken our physical body to the base octave and the soul or spiritual self to the top octave. If any note on the piano is sounded the string sets up a resonating vibration that causes the corresponding octave notes also to vibrate. If you play the middle 'C', every other 'C' note across all the octaves would start to sound. Indeed, within musical theory and experience, playing one note causes the harmonic notes also to sound. In this sense playing a note causes energy to be transferred across all the octaves of the piano.

Within us Ch'i can only be transferred through the different parts of our being if harmony exists. Without harmony a breakdown in the flow of Ch'i must occur. As the Tao states:

> *To live in harmony is to follow Tao.*
> *To follow Tao is enlightenment.*
> *Excessive striving*
> *Leads to exhaustion*
> *Competitive struggle*
> *Is contrary to Tao.*
> *Whatever contravenes Tao*
> *Will not endure.*
>
> (TAO 55)

Piano Metaphor

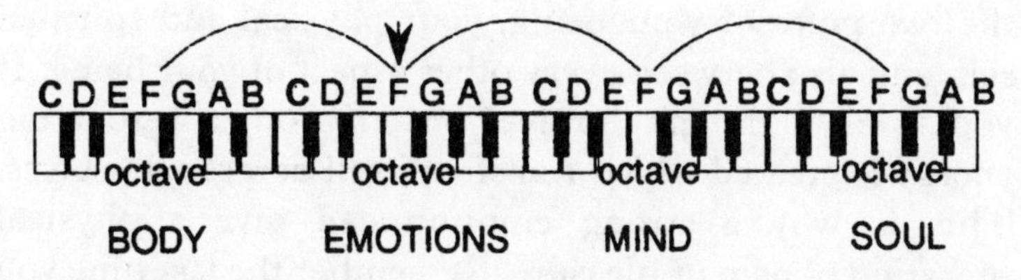

If the 'F' note of the emotions is sounded all other 'F' notes will resonate

This means that the body must be in harmony with the emotions, that must be in harmony with the mind, that must be in harmony with the spiritual self for Ch'i to flow through the whole system. If any note is off key or any part of us is in disharmony with the rest, a breakdown in the transmission of Ch'i occurs. We live in an imperfect world so there will always be minor imbalances in our circuits. By learning consciously to balance your energies you can do a great deal to maintain your health and vitality.

This principle of resonant connection can be visually demonstrated using a guitar, by placing a small piece of

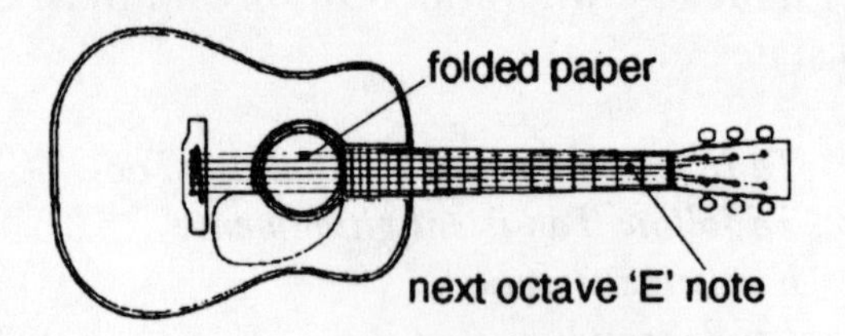

folded paper over the base string, which is generally pitched to the note 'E'. Even if this paper is placed over the centre hole of the guitar and a considerable sound is made by plucking the other strings the paper does not move. But when the next octave 'E' is plucked, the paper on the base string becomes violently agitated, indicating that the string is vibrating even though it has not been plucked itself.

In exactly the same way energy is transferred between the two poles of your being, your physical and spiritual self, and also between every other aspect of your being. If you think a thought or feel an emotion, a resonating energy is created which transfers itself across all octaves. This is why a strong emotion can give a physical sensation of pain or pleasure. Remember the last time you experienced a powerful emotion, what did you feel in your body? Did it bring tears to your eyes or a lump to your throat?

Understanding how this process works is one of the key elements for appreciating why psychosomatic problems occur, for negative thought patterns cause corresponding imbalances at a physical level. Conversely, food, drugs and other substances introduced into the body can affect your emotions and mind. There is a symphony playing within all parts of you at each moment of time. The key to life is allowing all your notes to play in tune and, what is more important, to play the music that is truly you. We need to discover those qualities that fully reflect our inner essence and then express them in ways that enrich others. As has been said disharmony

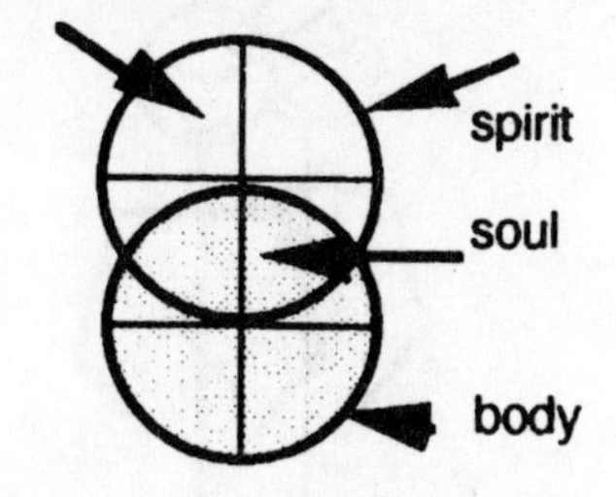

Link between body and spirit

occurs when, metaphorically, some of the notes get out of tune and we start to play discordantly. This causes a breakdown in the flow of energy through the system and consequently leads to all forms of dis-ease. Energy can only flow when the notes are pitched to the same resonant frequency, so if some part of you is out of tune with the rest a blockage must occur.

Suppose that your spiritual self wishes to express an artistic talent such as painting, but because of the pressures of work you keep rejecting this inner prompting. A tension then occurs between these two aspects of the self and the resultant disharmony will cause a breakdown in the flow of Ch'i through your being. If this imbalance is continually neglected it could eventually lead to some form of physical illness. Discovering your blockages is an important step on the way to vibrant health and inner fulfilment.

The Effects of Foods and Drugs

At the other end of the spectrum there have been many studies showing the different psychological and emotional effects of different foods and drugs taken into the body. This principle can be easily demonstrated. Most people have experienced drinking alcohol at some time or other in their lives. At an energetic level alcohol

Alcohol Intake

A separation starts to occur between the body and the spiritual self.

will start to change the rate of vibration of key elements within the physical body. Using the piano metaphor we could say that some of the base octave notes start to change frequency and when this happens, the flow of Ch'i from the higher frequencies is impeded. The first consequence is that you can initially feel more relaxed. It blocks out some of your inhibitions. Take more alcohol into the system and more notes become affected, causing eventually a greater dislocation to occur. This causes the spiritual self to start to lose control of the body, so that eventually, with enough alcohol, you will lapse into unconsciousness. Fortunately as alcohol is flushed from the system, everything returns to normal and full control is gained once more, but other types of non-medical drugs can have more lasting damaging effects. Sometimes this dis-location can occur for other reasons and many people have experienced the feeling of being disconnected from their body. It happens naturally in sleep state and 'flying' dreams are a memory of this experience.

Medicinal drugs, taken for psychological problems, can also have this blocking effect on the physical body. They allow mentally or psychically disturbed individuals to retain a level of balance in their lives. The difficulty here is that the drugs can sometimes be seen as the only method of control, rather than as a means of temporary relief. Ideally other forms of treatment are necessary to deal with the root cause of the problem that can lie on an emotional, mental or spiritual level.

In the nineteenth century the split between our mind and body was known as 'dualism', where each was seen as a separate entity. Modern researches into bio-chemistry and the workings of the brain have tended to discount this theory, for all thoughts can be seen to have a physical expression in brain's neuro-transmitter system. The quest to understand consciousness by many leading scientists, following this line of thinking, discounts any notion of 'dualism'. It is, of course, extremely difficult to separate out the 'pure' thought from its manifestation through the physical body. In the piano analogy, the difference in physical time between the moment when the top note 'C' is sounded and when all the other 'C' notes respond is the speed of sound. To all intents and purposes this is instantaneous. One area that does offer fruitful research in this respect is the 'near death experience' which will be discussed later in this chapter.

Because your thoughts are such an important aspect of your being, your belief structures play a crucial role in determining how your life unfolds. If you deny the existence of your spiritual nature, you immediately deprive yourself of an important source of sustenance and guidance. Similarly, you limit yourself if you believe strongly that you cannot achieve certain objectives. We all have the potential to develop and use our healing ability if we are open to the possibilities of what can be achieved. Christ said '**Seek and Ye shall find**'. It is also true to say that '**We find what we seek**'. Thus we need to be open and flexible, for strong fixed beliefs in any direction can easily lead us up blind alleys.

Understanding how Ch'i is exchanged between the different parts of yourself can give many valuable insights into patterns that make up your life. Physical illness arises either from acute conditions due to accidents or viral infections, or from long-term imbalances that cause chronic problems like arthritis or rheumatism. Western medicine is generally far better adapted to dealing with acute problems because it tends to approach health primarily at a physical level. It is much less successful with chronic conditions because these can very often arise from energy imbalances at an emotional, mental or spiritual level. However, many complementary systems treat these other levels, such as homoeopathy, acupuncture, radionics, psychotherapy and spiritual healing, to name but a few.

An example of the dynamic relationship between body, emotions, mind and spirit occurred with a friend of mine who contracted ME (chronic fatigue syndrome) within a few weeks of getting married and became completely incapacitated for a number of years. No treatment proved successful until she started to explore the spiritual side of her life. This led her to understand that there was a fundamental rift between the energy of herself and her husband and it was only when they finally separated that she regained full health and vitality.

When you are confronted by an illness or imbalance the challenge that faces you is to tackle the cause of the problem, not just treat the symptoms. Imbalances can occur on every level, of which physical illness is but one facet. Relationships are another important aspect in our lives and their health or otherwise can be judged in exactly the same way that we view physical illness. Indeed any part of us that is in a state of dis-ease within our being needs attention.

The first question you need to ask yourself is ***'What do I need to alter to restore health and balance?'*** To do this successfully you have to be open to change.

Polarity Balance Between Physical Body and Spiritual self

Body	*Physical body*	*Spiritual self*
Time Location	Fixed in linear time: time moves from the past to the future.	Circular time: past, present and future exist simultaneously. (Consciousness can access the past and future instantly.)
Space Location	Located at a specific place.	Exists everywhere simultaneously. (Consciousness can access any space instantly.)
Duration of Existence	Finite life – birth and death	Infinite life – no birth or death

This chart shows the new emerging explanation of the time and space relationship between the physical body and the spiritual self. It helps us understand how it is possible to foresee future events and the ability of the mind to send healing at a distance. The emotional body has a closer association with the physical body. The mental body has a closer association with the spiritual self. Through our thoughts we can remember the past and imagine the future: be aware of ourself in a specific place or imagine ourself at the other side of the world.

The Dynamics of the Psyche

To understand the causes of dis-ease and, conversely, what we need to do to find happiness and fulfilment, we need to understand the underlying patterns that make up our lives. There are three dominating forces that weave through every aspect of your life and shape you into who and what you are. These influences stem from:

- environmental experiences – **Ch'i**;
- genetic or hereditary patterns – **Jing**;
- the Ch'i of the spiritual self – **Shen**;

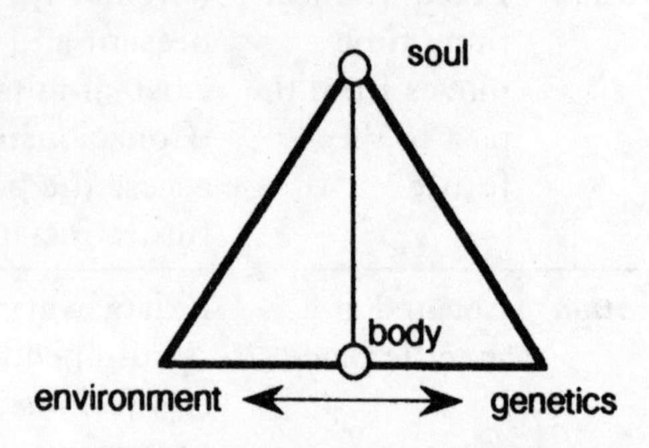

The three dominating life forces

The first two have long been recognised in scientific circles and have been the subject of much heated debate as to which is dominant; the **nature** versus **nurture** controversy. The third aspect has been little researched or considered in this equation but, as we shall see, it has a pivotal role in relation to the other two. In Ancient China these three elements were known as Ch'i, Jing and Shen. The concept of Ch'i has already been discussed, but broadly it can be said to equate with environmental forces. Jing is the energy that comes to us from our ancestors and also connects to sexual activity. Shen is the power from our spirit.

Environmental Influences

Environmental influences encompass everything that has happened to you throughout your life stemming from outside forces. These include relationships with other people as well as the more obvious environmental patterns like noise, pollution and the food we eat. Taken in a broader perspective they also involve more subtle influences like astrological patterns and some of the specific energies within the landscape like 'geopathic stress'.

Clearly experiences, particularly those in early childhood, have a powerful effect in shaping your character: 'Show me the child to the age of seven and I will show you the man' was the assertion of St Ignatius Loyola. Traumas in our childhood sometimes leave seemingly indelible imprints in our psyches that are very hard to eradicate. We all have had some difficult situations in our early years that, like the dropped stitch in knitting, creates a flaw in the pattern of our lives. Psychotherapy or counselling can be very important in helping us sort out some of these childhood problems, that so easily and repeatedly get triggered within. Yet upbringing in itself is not the sole answer. Indeed, advances in the realms of genetic engineering have shown how powerfully and diversely your genes shape your life.

Ancestral Patterns

Until recently it was assumed that genetic patterning was primarily responsible for our physical make-up, and had little to do with social behaviour or mental and emotional outlook. These patterns normally only became a problem when a genetic illness was passed on to the offspring. More recent studies have suggested that the genes may encode far more information than originally supposed. Family patterns and how to heal them may become as important an aspect of therapy as dealing with childhood traumas.

This new awareness of the power of hereditary patterns was triggered by recent research on identical twins who had been separated at birth and brought up in different family backgrounds. This began with a remarkable discovery around twin individuals called Jim Springer and Jim Lewis. The first in an amazing series of coincidences occurred when each twin was independently given the name Jim by his respective adoptive parents. This happened without any collusion between them. Each twin grew up separately, until they finally met again when they were 39. When they shared information on their respective lives they realised that there had been many more incredible parallel experiences.

Both Jim Springer and Jim Lewis had married girls called Linda, divorced them and then remarried women called Betty. Both had two sons whom they named, James and Allan, and James and Alan, the only difference being the spelling of Al(l)an. Both had owned a dog as a child and called it 'Toy'. Both used to holiday on the same beach in Florida (a stretch of sand only 300 yds long), driving there in the same type of car, a Chevrolet. Both bit their fingernails down to the quick and suffered tension headaches. Both chained-smoked Salem cigarettes. Both had worked part time as a deputy-sheriff; both had been attendants in filling stations and so on. There were many more coincidences that they shared.

Their story eventually came to the notice of Professor Bouchard from the University of Minneapolis who embarked upon his now famous study to discover other such twins and to look at the possible similarities. It was found that although Jim Springer and Jim Lewis's case was extraordinary, it was not unique.

All the evidence from these studies suggests that your genetic make-up plays a powerful role in determining some of the important patterns of your life, even to the extent of the lifestyle preferences that both Jims displayed. In other cases in the study, twins married at the same time, had injuries and illnesses at a similar period in their lives, as well as the more obvious similarities of choosing the same types of clothes.

Not all the identical twins studied displayed such extensive similarities as the Springer/Lewis twins. An additional factor, in their case, could be to do with the resonating telepathic connection that the twins unconsciously maintained between themselves. Subtle communication between the twins could have influenced them to act in similar ways, but forms of telepathic communication alone could not explain all the coincidences that occurred. Genetic patterning would appear to be the most obvious explanation.

Recent research suggests that while twins are 90 per cent the same physically they are only 35 per cent the same mentally. The propensity to stealing is thought to be 78 per cent genetic, while alcoholism is only 35 per cent. Studies into schizophrenia have revealed an interesting fact. In some cases it wold appear that the underlying cause is 100 per cent genetic, while in others it is solely down to environmental factors and in yet others it is a mixture between both. Clearly there is another factor at work here. I believe this relates to the impulses that stem from our spiritual self.

From the above studies it would seem likely that many of the patterns that shape your life stem from your genetic make-up and are not just determined by environmental factors. There are forms of healing coming forward today to do with integrating the Jing of our

'ancestors' on the basis that we are carrying some of their energy imbalances. This is an idea that is perhaps more fully understood in the Bible when it warns of the 'Sins of the fathers even unto the third and fourth generation'.

The Spiritual Self

The third aspect that provides a powerful dynamic to your life stems from your spiritual self or soul. This is the part that science neglects entirely but which, I suggest, plays a key role in the balance between the other two elements. The primary perceived function of the soul or spiritual self is to provide the motivating spark that keeps us alive and allows us to experience the physical world. However this is a limited view of its task for it suggests a very subservient role to the impact of genetics or the environment. By its very nature we cannot be dogmatic about its function, but enough clues, both scientific and anecdotal, are now available to give a greater comprehension of its role within the body.

The near death experience

A good starting point would be a consideration of the work of Dr Raymond Moody. He presented in his book *Life after Life* evidence for an experience that later became known as 'the near death experience' or NDE. Similar studies have validated his findings, since his initial research was published in 1975. Moody originally collected around 150 stories from people who had momentarily 'died' either from accident or physical illness. In these particular cases the individuals in question reported a remarkable and consistent inner experience. First, at the moment of trauma the consciousness of the person appeared to separate itself from the body and view what was taking place from another perspective. For example, in an operation, they might feel as though they were floating near the ceiling looking down at the medical staff trying to revive a body that for all purposes had just died. They could then find themselves travelling through a long tunnel towards a light and when they emerged they met people they knew who had already died. At this point a voice or a 'being of light' would tell them that it was not their time to pass over. They would then feel themselves being drawn back into their body and regaining consciousness.

One of the most startling elements of the near death experience is its profound effect upon the individuals concerned. In almost all circumstances they lose all fear of death, although not perhaps of dying. In the majority of cases it also radically changed their perspective on life, making them more tolerant and understanding of others. Many also reported very powerful feelings of peace and joy that accompanied these experiences. In a remarkable interview on the video *Visions of Hope*, Dr Elizabeth Kübler Ross demonstrated how she set about verifying the near death experience as a factual reality. Seeking out blind NDE people, who had lost their sight for at least ten years, she asked them to describe all that they had 'seen' when they were out of their bodies. She then set out to verify the factual accuracy of their reports. She found that these 'blind' people described exactly what took place, including the colours and types of the clothes that people were wearing. This is, of course, a physical impossibility in normal medical terms. These experiences bear witness to the powerful idea that our inner consciousness or spiritual self is not tied to the human body, but rather uses the body as a vehicle to express itself.

If our spiritual self can separate itself from the body and have an independent existence, we need to consider its function. If it can survive death it is reasonable to consider whether it existed prior to conception. Hypnosis and regression techniques have started to provide some clues to these tantalising questions. Over the past 20 years a number of people have recovered memories of previous lives, and these have been instrumental in healing physical, emotional and psychological problems. These experiences link with a worldwide belief in reincarnation found in many different religions and traditions. The researches of Professor Ian Stevenson and others have produced a number of cases that can only be satisfactorily explained in terms of past lives. Because of the extraordinary complexity of human existence, final proof may never be achieved, but a growing band of individuals are now looking successfully to past lives to resolve some of their present problems.

Reincarnation?

The belief in reincarnation suggests that we live a series of lives where some of the patterns that have not been fully integrated within the psyche get carried forward into the next life. Dr Roger Woolger in his book *Other Lives, Other Selves* describes many accounts of helping individuals release 'remembered' traumas from past lives. Having discovered the cause of their blockages, many of these people subsequently feel an important release in physical and emotional tension. In many cases a complete 'cure' occurred from what previously had been seen as an intractable condition.

For many years I used to bite my fingernails quite badly. Despite many attempts to stop, using all sorts of techniques, I was never successful until one particular day. Musing on the problem I had an inspiration to experiment with the idea of complementary opposites or polarities. 'If I am continually making my nails shorter by biting away at them what would happen if I imagined them growing longer and longer?' I thought. Sitting quietly, with my eyes closed, imagining this, I suddenly flipped into an altered state of consciousness. I was aware of myself experiencing a life in China where I had long nails. There long nails were a symbol of power and authority. Something about that life made me feel very uncomfortable, that I seemed to be unconsciously rejecting. This appeared to be why in this life I felt compelled to bite my nails. By just sitting quietly and accepting this energy, as part of me, with all its negative connotations, the desire to bite my nails completely went. From that moment it ceased to be a problem.

Many other people have had similar dramatic changes in their lives by simply unlocking a supposed past memory that was causing the problem. There is one other important point to note from the anecdotal evidence of people who have recovered these memories. Those who felt they had died traumatically, through being slain on a battlefield or whatever, often found some pattern or mark of their injuries on their present body. This could be in the form of birth marks or other bodily disfigurations that, in some cases, spontaneously occurred for no apparent reason at a particular age. It would seem that the mark or injury to the present body happened at the same age when the person died in a previous life.

In one particular case a friend had a problem that suddenly started at the age of eight and lasted for many years. She found for no apparent reason enormous blisters appearing on her body that were aggravated by jewellery and other metal objects. This problem was not relieved, despite all sorts of attempts using orthodox and unorthodox remedies, until many years later, when she 'remembered' being burnt alive at a similar age in a previous life. As soon as she had recovered this memory, the problem disappeared.

If this link between spirit and body can be established, and the evidence for it, by its very nature, must be speculative, then it supports a very important idea. This is that our spiritual self must be able to affect and mould the genetic structure and impose its patterning on the body. Taking this one stage further it underpins another powerful belief held by many who espouse the concept of reincarnation. It suggests that there is a level of choice in the life that we lead and in consequence responsibility for all that happens to us.

Research into the experiences of the developing foetus and pre-birth regression suggests that the link between the soul and fertilised egg occurs very early on, probably at the moment of conception. Once this connection is made a form of programming would appear to take place whereby the spiritual self sets in motion some of the key elements that need to come forward within a life. From the evidence of Professor Bouchard's findings it seems that this programming at a physical level is encoded within the DNA structure that provides an extensive blueprint for our lives. However, it is also clear that the spiritual self or soul can override this patterning, at least to a certain extent, which is why changes occur when past traumas are resolved.

Dr Rupert Sheldrake, in his theories on 'morphic resonance', has suggested an appropriate model that could explain this. He believes that our genetic structure, contrary to popular theory, is more akin to a television set, that is programmed to receive incoming information, rather than being its originator. This makes complete sense considering the above. In writing this book I am sitting at a computer terminal that is programmed to act in a certain way. If I push specific keys I know what functions will occur. For better or worse the computer will not write the book on its own. It needs me to input the information. I also know that the programs I hold in the computer will only allow me to do certain tasks. I cannot, for example, do complicated graphic work. I would need additional programs for this. In a similar way our spiritual self could activate or trigger off inbuilt programs when it chooses. In this way it could determine those experiences that it sees as a necessary part of its life pattern.

There is also another possible physical explanation of why changes occur. It is known that the DNA molecule, which cannot be changed, creates another molecule called RNA in order to instruct the body how to behave. It normally replicates itself precisely, but recent studies in animals have suggested that diet and the physical environment can change its structure. This suggests that instead of being immutable, the genes, like computer programs, can be rewritten.

Tied in with the belief in reincarnation is the idea that all experience is cumulative and the greater the number of experiences the higher the level of accomplishment of the individual in question. This is perhaps an explanation for child prodigies like Mozart and those individuals who have a very clear sense of their own destiny. Great spiritual teachers, like Jesus, Buddha, Mohammed, Moses and so on, could be seen as elder souls with much accumulated wisdom and experience behind them.

Karmic Patterns

Finally, in this chapter we need to look at the concept of karma. Traditionally karma, a belief from Hindu philosophy, was seen as the working out of the *'law of cause and effect'*. If an individual causes pain and suffering to a person in one life, they will have to atone for what was done when they return to a new body. In other words we reap what we sow. The idea of atonement is a central tenet of many religions, although usually it takes place in the next world, not in this. Perhaps a more enlightened way of understanding karma is to see it as a way of achieving wholeness. It would appear to involve a level of contrition from the evolving soul in order that it might continue to grow. However, experience from regression cases would suggest that it is possible for the soul to choose the way that it wishes to make up for what it has inflicted on others. So, for example, an individual who had been caught up in the tortures of the Inquisition could choose to come back as an invalid or as a person who is devoted to helping disabled people.

It should be emphasised that this does not imply that all who suffer some physical or mental defect do so because they have caused others suffering in a previous life. We must not forget Christ's comment to his disciples on the man born blind, when they asked 'Who did sin, this man or his parents, that he was born blind?' Jesus's reply was quite unequivocal when he answered 'Neither hath this man sinned, nor his parents: but that the works of God should be made manifest in him'. There can be many reasons why the spiritual self should choose to suffer some disability in a life. However, karma can also be seen as bringing forth positive benefits. If you help another, in whatever way, then that good will come back to you.

A strange experience highlighting the idea of karma and reincarnation occurred to me a few years ago. In my early 20s I knew a delightful middle-aged lady who was also a remarkable clairvoyant. She mentioned to me one day that she could see me, in a former life, being guillotined in the French Revolution. She claimed this was one of the reasons that I suffered tension headaches that stemmed from the back of my neck (which was true). I can recall at the time feeling that this might well be possible. Although I had not had a direct inner experience or memory of living in that period, I always felt very uncomfortable when I read anything about the French Revolution or saw films on the subject. Many years later I had an induced regressed memory of a life at that time. Shortly after this I had an opportunity to go to Paris. It was a period in my life when I was sifting through a number of problems. It therefore seemed appropriate to spend some of my time there visiting the sites connected with the Revolution. When walking through the streets of Paris, I had a much more tangible feeling of being there in a former life, although previous suggestions could have caused this.

To lay to rest any difficult karma from that time I felt it appropriate to send out thoughts of forgiveness in a symbolic sense to all who had caused me pain and suffering. This went well until I reached the Place de la Concorde, which is where the executions took place. Sitting quietly to send out these thoughts of forgiveness and healing I was suddenly struck by the thought, 'Why did I choose to be guillotined?' Like a bolt from the blue an immediate answer came back, 'Because you were responsible for cutting off other people's heads in an earlier life'. The power of this thought was so strong that I could not doubt its veracity. To heal this situation, I sensed that I had to ask inwardly for forgiveness from any person I had similarly harmed. And this is what I did.

The final twist to this tale happened about six months later when I met someone on a healing course. Something powerful happened in the interaction between us and, that evening, he spontaneously regressed back into a life in China where he thought I had been responsible for having his head cut off. A few days later we met up and he described his traumatic experiences concluding his conversation with, 'I just want to say I forgive you'. The power of that moment was electric. I was then able to share with him my own experiences from Paris.

Taken on their own these three incidents of biting my nails, 'remembering' a life in the French Revolution and the connection with another who 'remembered' a life in China might not amount to much. Taken together they create a powerful picture that has a wonderful completeness about it. It just feels right; not scientific perhaps but anecdotally very potent.

This case illustrates some simple ways that you can heal imbalances from a past life if you suspect this to be a cause of a problem. To delve deeper you might need to seek the aid of a therapist who specialises in this field but this is not always necessary.

Forgiveness

Forgiveness is one of the most powerful tools for letting go of past trauma. To be effective it needs to be done in three ways: to forgive others for what they have done to you; to ask for forgiveness for what you have done to others; and above all to forgive yourself. This is perhaps the hardest part of all.

There needs to be one word of caution in delving willy-nilly into our past lives for idle curiosity. There is clearly a very good reason why we do not easily remember our previous existences. A little careful thought reveals why this is so. Each life produces a flavour of Ch'i that is appropriate to the life in question. When we incarnate we draw upon this reservoir of experience to select those energies that are most appropriate for us, rather like a painter selecting certain colours for a painting. If we link into past lives in an inappropriate way we could draw specific energies to us that are not relevant to this present life, like spilling a pot of red paint over a picture of an oak tree. The two do not blend easily together.

There are two criteria that can help us determine what is appropriate and what is not. First, has the memory occurred spontaneously without any specific delving? I was not thinking about past lives when I was working on my fingernails. Secondly, has the problem failed to respond to any other treatment from this life? If you have conscientiously sought a solution through the many therapies that are at present available to you and nothing has been resolved, then working on a previous existence may be a valid option.

To find balance in our lives we need to be open to possibilities of the origins of dis-ease. It is not necessary to have a belief in reincarnation to be a good healer or to lead a fulfilled life. It is only relevant if it helps you find greater harmony within. The Tao tell us:

> *Wise people seek solutions;*
> *The ignorant only spread blame.*
> (TAO 79)

The following exercise is designed to bring forward a quality of forgiveness. It may need to be repeated in some instances, particularly in those cases where you have felt very hurt or betrayed by another. In all these cases you need to consider why you should have attracted such a situation into your life. We all, at some stage of our lives, will need to forgive someone else. It is one of the most powerful healing exercises that can be undertaken. The Tao informs us:

> *There is no greater tragedy*
> *Than making enemies*
> *For then you lose your treasure,*
> *Your peace.*
> *When conflict arises,*
> *Compassion always prevails.*
>
> (TAO 69)

EXERCISE

Practising Forgiveness

(fifteen minutes)

Sit comfortably in an upright chair or cross-legged on a cushion if you prefer. Close your eyes and for a few moments focus on your breathing. Then sense a connection to the spiritual self within. Now carry out the following procedure:

- Think of the person whom you wish to forgive and affirm in your thought 'I forgive you for all that you have inflicted upon me'. Try to really feel and mean this.
- Next send out a thought asking for forgiveness from any person that you have similarly harmed. You might feel that you could not have done such a thing to a person as has been done to you, but remember this could have happened in a past life. You could say to yourself 'I ask for forgiveness for any person that I have inadvertently harmed.'

- Finally bring your thoughts back to yourself and say inwardly 'I forgive myself for acting in a hurtful way towards others and for the mistakes that I have made'.

When you have completed this bring yourself back to waking consciousness and open your eyes. You might then like to write down anything that you sensed or felt.

To follow Tao brings compassion.
Compassion leads to tolerance.
Tolerance brings strength.
Strength means harmony with nature;
Harmony with nature means oneness with Tao.
One with Tao, you are empowered
And your life will be free from harm.

(TAO 16)

Summary

- The most dense level of our energy field is the physical body. The finest level is our soul or spiritual self.
- Energy will travel across octaves so that all layers of our being are interconnected. The physical body affects the spirit and vice versa.
- Our thoughts and emotions are different layers of our energy field.
- There are three driving energies that operate within every life. These stem from environmental influences, genetic patterning and the power of your spiritual self.

- The spiritual self is linked to the physical body but separates itself at death.
- The spiritual self would appear to programme the genetic structure to bring forward those experiences that it wishes to express.
- It is useful to work with the idea that the soul undergoes a number of lives as part of its cycle of experience.
- Forgiveness is one of the most powerful tools for letting go of past trauma.

CHAPTER 3

Meditation And Ch'i Balancing

Let your roots go deep into the source.
With insight build a firm foundation
Of peace in the Tao.

(TAO 59)

The Systems of Meditation

All life is based upon a weaving together of energy between the spiritual and physical worlds. Within the majority of people the greatest level of awareness is of the material world in which we reside. This is important, because the primary reason for being in a physical body is to learn about physical reality. This means that we are not generally very conscious of the spiritual realm and the importance it plays in life. Those who embark upon a study of healing, either from the basis of how they can help others or just how they can help themselves, need to address this aspect. It is important to begin to access into your spiritual self so that you can harmonise with the dictates of your inner being. There are a number of tried and tested ways that can help you achieve this objective. They include the use of prayer, meditation, listening to certain forms of music and dream interpretation. In this chapter we will focus on different meditative techniques and the role they can play in your spiritual life.

There are many different systems of meditation, some very ancient and others that have been developed over recent years. The fundamental goal of all meditation should be to help integrate the spiritual dimension into your life. Within many people there can be a split within the psyche, between the spiritual self and the Ego mind. The spiritual self has one set of objectives and the Ego self another. The great myth of Isis and Osiris from Ancient Egypt highlights this problem. Meditation can help us bridge this divide so that both mind and spiritual self function as one.

The Myth of Isis and Osiris

Osiris was a wise philosopher king who ruled Ancient Egypt with his consort Isis. He brought forward all the benefits of civilisation and agriculture to his people. He eventually determined that this knowledge should be made available to the rest of humanity, so he set off on a journey to achieve this.

While he was away his wicked brother Set wished to take over Egypt for himself, so he planned to trick and kill Osiris on his return. He did this by building a sarcophagus designed to the exact size of his brother.

When Osiris returned Set held a magnificent banquet in his honour and then promised to give the sarcophagus to whomever if fitted exactly. Eventually Osiris lay down in the sarcophagus, and at that moment Set rushed up and sealed the lid, then threw the sarcophagus into the Nile. He then took over the kingdom of Osiris. Isis was distraught and went in search of her husband, eventually finding his body. However, before she could bring him back to life Set found the two of them and this time cut the body of Osiris into 14 pieces, which he scattered throughout Egypt.

Once more Isis went in search of her husband, and collected all the parts together, except his penis, which had been eaten by a Nile crab. She breathed life back into Osiris, but he determined that from then on he would rule now only from the spiritual realm. It is left to Horus, the son of Osiris, the falcon-headed god, to fight Set on behalf of his father.

The myth can be interpreted on many levels but in principle tells of the split between the materialistic side of our nature (Set) and the spiritual part (Osiris). It is Isis (Love) that reconnects us to this spiritual aspect within.

Broadly speaking meditation techniques can be classified into the two categories of active or passive, sometimes referred to as yang and yin. What does this mean? Yang (active) meditations work with the mind in a creative way, often using symbolic images to access into the deeper layers of consciousness. Prayer is really a form of active meditation. Yin meditations try to put the mind into a very passive state so that the deeper impressions of the soul merge with our consciousness. Both types of meditations have their place; one is not better than the other. Ultimately you need to find those systems that best suit your temperament. This is very important and will depend upon a number of factors. As a generalisation the Eastern approach to spiritual seeking tends to be passive, while in the West the active is more predominant. This means that seeking within and exploring the inner life tends to be more developed in the East, while doing good works and helping others is more strongly emphasised in the West. The Eastern mind therefore is better adapted to passive systems of meditation while active systems are more suitable for the Westerner. However each person is an individual and a person living in the West may have had a number of incarnations in the East, perhaps India, China or Tibet. They will therefore naturally favour those cultures and religious systems for their spiritual expression.

This may partly explain why there has been a breakdown in traditional religious belief in the West. Many people are turning to practices like yoga, T'ai Ch'i and such like to express their spirituality. Indeed today we stand at a unique place in our spiritual development. Never before in the history of the world has there been such a wide diversity of religious traditions available to us. At any moment you could pick up a book or find a teacher to instruct you in Native American Indian traditions, Aboriginal traditions, Buddhism, Hinduism, Confucianism, yoga, Ch'i Kung, Ancient Egyptian or Nordic traditions, Christianity, Kabbalah and so on. Almost every type of spiritual development system that there has been over the past 5000 years is available to you. This is a wonderfully rich gift that should be welcomed with open arms, for it allows you an opportunity to connect to those times and cultures which illuminated and highlighted the spiritual side of your make-up.

The Importance of Meditation in Your Life

I once had the opportunity of interviewing Drukchen Rinpoche, a lama from Tibet, who perceives himself a direct incarnation of Avolokitsvara, the Tibetan Buddha of Compassion. In China this Buddha became transformed into the goddess of compassion called Kwan-Yin.

Asking Drukchen about meditation he affirmed its importance in the spiritual life. Questioning him further on how long we should meditate he said surprisingly, 'No more than five minutes per day'. Going on he said 'People are crazy and meditation can make you more crazy'. The most important aspect of meditation for him was holding the focus of your mind on what it is that you are meditating upon. Far better, he said, to spend 5 minutes of concentrated thought than 50 minutes in mindless drift. Meditation does not therefore need to take up a long period in your life, but can be very easily incorporated into your time schedules. Normally I will spend five minutes every morning and evening in meditation and only extend this period if there is specific information that I am trying to access, understand or balance within me. Indeed, seen at another level, if meditation is directed to allowing the spiritual self full expression within us, then our whole life can become a form of meditation.

Some Meditation Exercises

The exercises given below are but a tiny selection from a vast array of the different techniques that are available to you. They predominantly reflect an active approach to meditation. This has been done for two reasons. First, most of the readers of this book will express Western consciousness. Secondly, the passive systems of meditation are so well developed that literature and teachers abound in this area.

All the time we need to seek balance within. There can be periods of your life where one form of meditation is appropriate. You may then reach a point when you need to move on. Do not become trapped into thinking that there is only one correct system. If you are using a particular method and it ceases to provide balance then try another system. Do not be frightened of experimentation for this is how you grow.

Within the exercises given below will be some specifically geared to balancing your Ch'i. These can be incorporated as part of general self-healing exercises. These exercises are graduated in that the early ones provide a platform to which the others can be added.

EXERCISE

Basic Body Awareness

(three to five minutes)

Aim: *To provide body awareness for general Ch'i balancing.*

Adopt one of the following postures.

1. Sit in an upright chair, with a straight back, feet uncrossed and resting on the floor, and hands palms down on your thighs.
2. Sit cross-legged on a cushion or seat, in a 'lotus posture' if you can manage it, with palms facing up, but linking the thumb and first finger together.
3. Kneel using a meditation stool, and again link your thumb and index finger.

It is important to keep your back straight and not to slump down.

(**Note**: Different hand positions, known as Mudras, reflect different aims in meditation. Linking the thumb with the first finger symbolically connects the spiritual self with the 'Ego' consciousness.)

- Begin by closing your eyes and taking a few slightly deeper breaths, drawing the air right down into your abdomen. In doing this feel that you are relaxing yourself.

- Then direct your attention to your toes. Try and be fully aware of each toe in turn. If you can imagine it, try and sense how your toes would view the rest of you. This suggests that our toes are conscious, which of course they are. Feel that all the energy around your toes is balanced and flowing in a harmonious way.
- Next, slowly move your consciousness from your toes to your feet carrying out the same process, and then on up your body, focusing on each part in turn.
- When you reach your eyes, pause and then focus on a spot between and slightly about your eyes. This is known as the 'third eye' centre. This is one of the major control centres of the body and can be used for balancing your energies. Imagine, if you can, that your whole consciousness is centred on this spot and then sense that all the energies within you are balanced and harmonious. Hold this thought for a few moments, before bringing yourself back to full waking consciousness.

Go back to the beginning of the exercise if at any moment your mind starts to wander into other areas. If, for example, you reach your knees and then find you start to think about someone's knee problems, take your thoughts back to your toes and start all over again. This will begin to discipline your mind, which has often been seen as a monkey, leaping from idea to idea. We need gently to tame this monkey, so that it comes under our control. It does not matter in this case that you do not reach the brow, for it is the discipline that is important. Nor is this a test to see how quickly or slowly you can carry out this exercise. Meditation takes practice and unfortunately there are no short cuts.

EXERCISE

Connecting to Your Inner Light

(*five minutes*)

Aim: *The inner light is a reflection of your spiritual self. This is one of the easiest ways to connect to your inner source.*

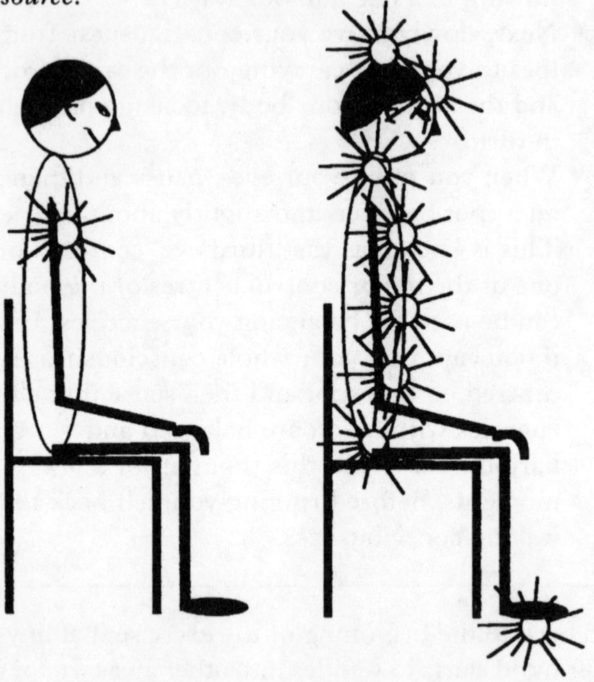

Connecting to your inner light

Different locations for your inner light

- Sit in one of the postures mentioned above and close your eyes.
- Carry out the **body awareness exercise** mentioned above. With practice this can be shortened to one to two minutes.

- When you have spent a few moments balancing the energies of your 'third eye' or 'brow centre', think of your inner spiritual self and try to sense, visualise, or feel this as a tiny flame of light.
- Assess where you have located it within your body and then slowly move your consciousness into the flame, so that you become the light and it becomes you.
- Hold that thought for a few moments before withdrawing and then slowly bringing yourself back to full waking reality.

(**Note**: If you fear fire you could use another symbol for your spiritual self. A golden chalice would be a good alternative.)

Write down any impressions that you gained. You can also carry out a number of supplementary exercises.

- First, when you have located your light try moving it into different parts of your body, and see what you feel and experience. If, for example, you originally felt it was within your heart, move it up to your head, and then enter into its light.
- Second, you can locate the light in your heart area and then imagine its radiance is permeating your physical body. Then sense it extending out into your energy fields, so that you are totally encompassed in its Ch'i. Try then to see the light getting brighter and brighter.

When you have completed this exercise slowly bring yourself back to full waking consciousness.

(**Warning**: There is sometimes a tendency to seek this light outside of yourself, i.e. in some space above your head. The challenge of being in a physical body is to ground and earth the spiritual aspect within you. If you project your consciousness out of the body there is a danger of splitting off part of your psyche. The effect of this will mean that it becomes difficult to balance your energies within the physical. This is why meditating for long periods of time is often not desirable, for the meditation can become a form of cop-out from normal living. Remember Drukchen's advice. Therefore try not to project yourself into any light or spiritual space that is outside of you. Rather bring that light, your spiritual self, fully into you, before connecting with it.)

EXERCISE

Strengthen Your Concentration

(*three to five minutes*)

Aim: *To strengthen your concentration and visualisation ability.*

You will require a candle and timer for this exercise.

- Light the candle and sit in one of the poses given above.
- Set the timer for two minutes.
- With your eyes open focus your mind on the candle as a shape and object only. Observe its colours, the energy of the flame and how it relates to the background, but nothing else. If your mind starts to wander off or make connections to other things, gently bring it back to holding attention on the candle. If you are

unused to doing this the two minutes will seem a long time.

- When the two minutes are completed re-establish contact with your normal waking mode.
- Now set the timer again for two minutes, but this time in looking at the candle allow your mind to contemplate how it was made, what candles are used for, why they are often part of religious rites, what they symbolise etc. Allow whatever associations come up to be explored but also keep coming back to the candle.
- When the two minutes are up once more re-establish contact with your normal waking mode.
- Finally set the time again, but this time close your eyes, and try and visualise the candle for two minutes. If the image starts to fade, briefly open your eyes, look at it again and then repeat trying to visualise it.
- Once again re-establish contact with your normal waking mode when the time is up.

Write down your impressions.

If you carry out any of these exercises within a group, share your experiences, for it can be very valuable perceiving others' insights.

This type of exercise can be carried out with many different types of objects; a pencil, your hand, a piece of sculpture to name but a few. When you feel ready you can extend the time of each session to three, four or five minutes. This will help your healing work and strengthen your ability to hold the focus of your attention at will.

EXERCISE

Ch'i Balancing

(three to five minutes)

Aim: *This exercise can be used to balance and circulate energy throughout your being.*

Drawing Ch'i from the earth

Drawing Ch'i from the sky

- Adopt your normal meditation pose and carry out the **body awareness exercise**.
- Imagine, sense or feel that there is an energy within the earth and gently feel that you are drawing this up your spine, through to the crown of your head. You might like to see this energy as a coloured light.

- When the energy reaches your head, feel that it is showering out around and through your aura back to the ground, and from there back up your spine once more, rather as though you are a fountain.
- With a little practice it should being to feel as though there is a continuous loop of energy travelling through and around you all the time.
- After a few minutes reverse this process and imagine that you are drawing energy down from the cosmos through the top of your head and down your spine into the earth.
- Then let the energy shower up through your surrounding energy field to the top of your head, before it travels down your spine once more.
- Once more hold this thought for a few minutes, feeling the energy is washing through every part of your energy field.
- Finally sense that everything is brought to a standstill and that you have de-linked from these energy flows. Gently re-establish connection back with your normal waking consciousness.

EXERCISE

Balancing the Yang/Yin Polarity

(five minutes)

***Aim**: To balance the masculine/feminine aspects of yourself.*

Ideally this exercise is best carried out on a sofa or with three chairs.

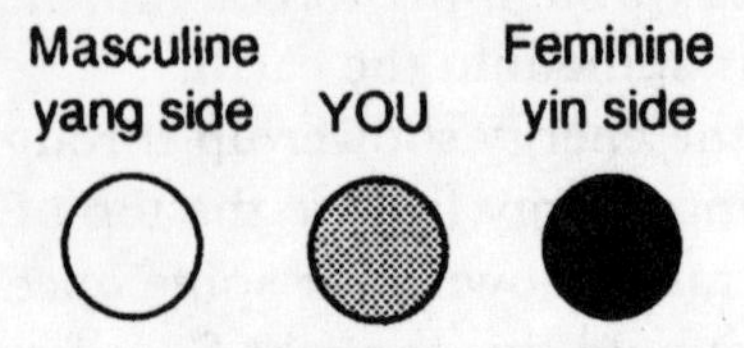

*Determine which is your yang side and which is your yin side. Then imagine that you are sitting in each aspect in turn. Then blend these two energies to form **Vesica Pisces**.*

Vesica Pisces symbol

- Sit in the middle of the sofa or the middle of the three chairs and carry out the **body awareness exercise**, then connect with your **inner light**.
- Ask within which side of you represents your masculine or yang polarity and which represents your feminine or yin side. Imagine that these two energies are like two globes or spheres of colour on either side of you. Try and see, sense or feel them as clearly as you can.
- Now physically move your position into one or other of the two spheres. Try and fully experience the quality of energy that it contains.
- Next, move into the opposite polarity and once more feel into the quality of its energy. How does your masculine side express itself and how does your feminine side express itself?
- Now move back to the centre, and try and imagine these two globes coming together so that they interlock as a Vesica Pisces symbol (where the centre of one circle is on the circumference of the other). Try and sense the balance between these two aspects.
- Finally bring yourself back to normal waking consciousness.

With a little practice it becomes possible to do this exercise without moving, but repositioning yourself helps reinforce the quality of balance.

This type of exercise can be used for all types of polarity balancing. You could explore your emotions by putting joy on one side and sadness on the other or anger on one side and peace on the other. Alternatively, you could work with it to balance the light and shadow sides of your nature.

EXERCISE

Merging Meditation

(five minutes)

***Aim**: To give greater awareness of other life forms in nature and how they relate to you. In this exercise a tree is chosen but any aspect of nature can be used.*

- Adopt your normal meditation pose, close your eyes and carry out the **body awareness exercise.**
- Next imagine that you are standing in front of a tree. You have no shoes or stockings on so that you can feel the ground beneath your feet. Be aware of any sounds that you can hear, of birds or insects. There is a gentle breeze blowing and you can feel its soft caress on your cheek. Look at the tree, its shape and size. What type of tree is it? Now move closer and feel its bark. Is it rough or smooth?
- Next turn your back to the tree and feel yourself leaning against it. What feelings do you get from this tree? What is this type of tree used for? Can you see the processes of its use in your mind?
- Now finally let yourself start to merge with the tree, so that you become it and it becomes you, feeling up into its branches and down to the roots. What do you experience now? Allow yourself to be in this space for a minute or two, before disengaging. See yourself once more as separate from the tree standing looking at it. Then let the picture fade from your mind, be aware of yourself again in the room and open your eyes.
- Write down what you have experienced.

This type of meditation can provide wonderful insights into many aspects of life. You can use this form of identification exercise with almost anything, such as animals, plants, buildings (pyramid), people (Christ/Buddha), fish, stars, symbols and so on. The mind has an infinite capacity to bring forth all sorts of associations and perceptions that can be of real value in helping us link with the spiritual side of ourselves.

Light and shadow

A word of warning should be given at this point. We are all a composition between light and shadow, the balanced and the chaotic sides of ourselves. Both are important in our evolutionary development. You should never try to run away from those aspects that you find disagreeable within, for if you do they are liable to overwhelm you in one way or another. The shadow contains all the unacknowledged parts of yourself, as well as those aspects like anger, greed, fear and so on. Sometimes, when carrying out any meditation the shadow elements will emerge. Do not be frightened of them. Acknowledge them, experience them but do not identify with them. Underlying all destructive emotions is fear in one form or another. To be whole you cannot run away from this fear. In truth the only thing you have to fear is the fear itself. Sit with it and move through it.

If, in carrying out any exercise, you hit on an aspect that brings up fear carry out the following procedure. Connect with your light within, then try and allow yourself to experience the fear fully, trying to understand its nature and the reason for it coming up. Then move on to the next stage of the meditation, all the time feeling the connection with the light within. If you can be brave enough to allow yourself to move through your fears it will have a profound effect on your life. This takes courage.

Problems of this sort do not often occur in meditation

but if they do it is much better to deal with them on an imagery/feeling level than letting them leak out in everyday life.

EXERCISE

Quiet Place Meditation

(five minutes)

***Aim**: This meditation exercise is designed to help you find peace and tranquillity within.*

To gain greatest benefit from carrying out any of these types of meditation is to bring into play as many of your physical senses as you can. If you can draw upon at least three of your senses, say touch, sight and hearing, then the focus of your mind will be held to the meditation image.

- Think of a place, either in the country or by the sea, where you have felt very calm and peaceful. Visualise yourself back at that place experiencing all that you did before. Look around and try and see everything as it was then. Listen out for any sounds of birds or insects and the smell of grass or flowers that you have experienced. Above all, use your sense of touch to feel the bark of any trees, the lapping water on the ground beneath you.
- Adopt your normal meditation posture, close your eyes and carry out your **body awareness exercise.**
- Now imagine that you are sitting or walking in this place of tranquillity. Use as many of your physical senses as you can. Above all, recall the feeling of peace and tranquillity that you

experienced, and allow it to permeate every cell of your body.

- When you feel you have been in this state for a few minutes, slowly disengage and bring yourself back to full waking consciousness.

The above meditations can be safely used on your own or within a group. If you are in a group one member can lead the others through these meditations. You could take turns to do this.

Some meditation practices are best undertaken under the guidance of a recognised teacher. Use your discrimination to decide what is right for you.

One of the most widely known forms of meditation is TM (transcendental meditation). This is based on using a mantra, a sound or word that is repeated over and over again. Repetition of a word in this way causes the conscious mind to freeze out, allowing for access into a deeper layer of our consciousness. It is a very simple form of meditation and can, if not overdone, provide excellent relief from some of the pressures of life. Studies have shown that any word can be used, like peace or love – apparently Lord Tennyson went into states of ecstasy by simply repeating his own name!

However, if overdone this type of meditation can sometimes cause a feeling of separation or disconnection from the body. This is not a desirable state as we saw above. If this is happening to you it is better to desist from this particular practice and try another approach.

Those techniques do not have to be restricted to your own home or meditation centre. If you are in the country or by the sea, find a quiet place to attune within and sense the connection with the spiritual energies that interweave in that place. For example, the tree meditation can be used with a real tree. Indeed, if you are feeling run down or emotionally drained, connecting with a tree can be one of the most beneficial forms of healing. Trees contain powerful spiritual energies, so respect them and make use of them. After all the Buddha obtained enlightenment under a tree, so why shouldn't you?

EXERCISE

Grounding Your Energies

(five minutes)

Aim: *To close down and earth your energies after any healing, psychic work or meditation.*

- After completing any exercise spend a few moments feeling centred and balanced within yourself.
- Imagine that the energy of your being is linked down into the earth like the roots of a tree and that you have grounded any excess energy.
- Bring yourself back to full waking consciousness, stretch and move around.

Summary

- Meditation is a valuable way to access into your spiritual self.
- There are many different meditation techniques. You need to find the systems that best suit your nature.
- Meditation techniques can be broadly classified as active or passive. Generally, active meditations are best suited to a Western mind.
- Meditation does not need to take up a long period each day – five to ten minutes is all that should be necessary.

- Rather than projecting your consciousness out of your body, try all the time to draw the spiritual world down into yourself.

CHAPTER 4

Protection And The Subtle Energy Fields of the Body

Deal with the complex
While it is still simple.
Solve large problems
While they are still small.

(TAO 63)

Protection

Protection is such a natural part of our daily experience that we rarely give it much thought. Your immune system protects your health, your clothes protect you from the weather and your home, among other things, protects your privacy, providing you with an ambient space in which to live. To operate safely and successfully on a healing level you also need to incorporate the concept of protection into your activities. Learning Ch'i protection is one of the most important aspects in maintaining health and vitality. There is an ancient Hermetic maxim 'As above, so below'. This implies that there are underlying principles which operate at every level within the cosmos and if we neglect them we do so to our cost. We can liken it to wearing seat belts in cars; they might seem an unnecessary inconvenience until we are involved in an accident.

On a physical level your basic protection is the skin of your body. Yet, on its own, this is rarely sufficient, so you wear clothes. The type of dress you wear is determined by the conditions that you expect to encounter, which vary considerably from season to season. If you wished to sunbathe it would be a necessary precaution to apply suntan oil. It is not that the sun is bad, on the contrary, but over-exposure to a strong energy can cause considerable suffering, unless you have built up an immunity to it. The same principle applies in healing and psychic work. With experience you can learn to use a wide variety of different protections, depending upon the type of work in which you are engaged. Providing the necessary precautions are taken only benefit can occur.

The Aura

Our Psychic Protection

We all have a natural protective barrier on a psychic level which is our **'aura'**. As well as reflecting different states of your health that healers can learn to interpret, your aura carries this most important function of protection. It is like a non-physical skin which generally operates very efficiently without any consideration. However, in developing your healing gifts you are in effect creating openings in this skin, like knocking new holes in the walls of your house. To complete the job you need to put in new doors and windows which you can learn to open and close at will.

The aura is a resonating energy field that surrounds us and functions rather like the earth's atmosphere. Meteorites winging towards the earth from outer space get frizzled up before they do any damage and the balance of gases cuts out harmful solar radiation.

Life, as we know it on this planet, would be impossible

without the atmosphere and similarly physical incarnation would be impossible without your auric protection. The difference between the two functions is that your aura encompasses all the non-physical levels of your being, including your thoughts and emotions. Its primary task is to cut out or detune those resonances that are not in harmony with you and could impair the integrity of your being. Without this protection it would be like trying to travel up a crowded one-way street in the wrong direction. You would be continually jostled by all those coming the opposite way. When properly balanced this protection permits the different parts of you to communicate together without undue outside interference.

The natural strength or resilience of your protection is dependent upon a number of factors. Some people's Ch'i fields are very strong and robust, while others are much more sensitive. It is weakened in ill-health and in states of dis-ease. The depletion of this energy field can be an indication of potential physical illness. All training which induces a quality of sensitivity to the energies of others will weaken its protective quality. This is why therapists can sometimes have health problems, unless measures are taken to counteract this.

Nature and Size of the Aura

There has been much debate in healing and psychic circles about the nature and size of the aura. Some suggest that it extends for several yards around us, while others think that it is less than a foot. It is claimed that the aura of the Buddha extended for several miles, but in some senses this is missing the point, for the spiritual part of us is not fixed in time or space. However, for convenience and to help focus your mind it is helpful to set a limit on what you imagine your aura to be. In this sense feeling that it extends completely around our bodies to a distance of about 2 ft is a good compromise.

You do not have to 'see' or visualise this energy field, just having a sense of it is sufficient.

We have already seen that when two things start to resonate or vibrate together an energy interchange occurs. This energy flows from the strongest to the weakest. Your aura acts as a barrier to these energies, but sometimes it is not strong enough to counteract powerful energies which can then become overwhelming. The dynamic forces generated in large crowds focused on a single objective can cause individuals to be swept into an emotional fervour sometimes against their better judgement. The emotions whipped up in pop concerts or football crowds are a good example of this. Such experiences are not in themselves wrong, but it is preferable to be able to choose whether you wish to participate or not. Your emotions are particularly vulnerable in this area. If you think about the different experiences in your life it is often possible to pick out those occasions when you acted out of character through the strong influence of another individual. Situations of anger, enthusiasm, depression or elation are often generated in this way. Some people easily become chameleons to the moods of others.

Spiritual Teachers

On another level, the inner reason to seek out a 'guru' or spiritual teacher is not what he or she can tell you, but what they can help you experience, by awakening through resonance those dormant aspects of yourself. This is known as *'Darshan'* in Buddhist traditions. A true teacher at this level is able to sound an inner note that can awaken the corresponding quality within you. If you can retain that note, or vibration, it will eventually become part of your life. The more conscious you can become the more you can determine the facets that you wish to become part of you. In these cases a healthy aura will allow you to assimilate this resonant energy in the most beneficial way.

Finding Harmony

If you wished to meditate, it would be foolish to choose the middle of a busy London street. It might be possible in the centre of one of London's parks, but is much more likely to be successful if you were within the confines of a building away from the hubbub of the metropolis, in a quiet place that protects you from noisy interference. By psychically protecting yourself you in effect create an inner space, a quiet sanctuary, that cuts out all extraneous 'psychic' noise and interference.

Developing your healing and receptive gifts heightens your perception to the vibrations or resonances of people and places. Places are important because they accumulate all the memories of things that have happened there. The more sensitive you become the more you will detect the different qualities of feeling that can be found in properties, rather like a cook learning to discriminate between the subtle flavours of a culinary feast.

Some individuals and places will be in harmony with you, and some will not. It is the energy from the latter that we need to be mindful of, for if that energy is appreciably stronger than you it can influence you adversely. However, you can easily counter this by learning to use appropriate protections. It is no different from choosing correct clothing in accordance with the weather. The healer who cannot shop in a supermarket or travel on the underground in the rush hour is not applying these principles to his or her life. Strengthening your protection should be no harder than deciding which suit of clothes you are going to wear for any set occasion. It is true that some find this harder than others, but then we are all unique and with practice we can all be successful.

Added Protection

As the aura is your natural protective mechanism you need to learn to draw additional qualities into or around

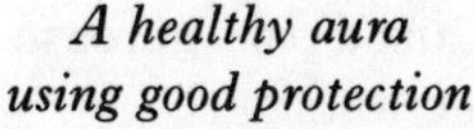

A healthy aura using good protection

An unhealthy aura with little or no protection

your aura to strengthen what is already there. You can do this in two ways, either by using your mind to create additional protections or by using physical objects that have acquired a protective association. If you wear the Christian cross in the belief that it is helping to protect you then immediately you open yourself to the potential of that protection. This creates a link with all those who have used the cross in a similar way. It is as though we tap into the collective unconscious, through the symbol, which invokes a powerful protective energy. But, instead of wearing a physical cross, you could with greater success use a visual image of the cross imposed on part or the whole of your body. Indeed, the two systems can work well together, for at times we need both. Symbols like the cross help focus our attention and, used in conjunction with ritual, such as in the Catholic mass, can invoke powerful energies. But situations do not always allow us to work with physical symbols, so learning to use imagery is also important

Three colours have traditionally been used for protection – white, blue and gold. They each carry slightly different flavours and it is of value to practise using each of them. Which one you finally settle for will be dependent upon your situation and what you feel most comfortable with. White reflects back light and has a mirroring effect on what is projected at it. As a blending of all colours it contains both yang and yin energy. Blue, as in the cloak of the Madonna, is associated with the feminine and the quality of spiritual love. It reflects the yin principle on a spiritual level. Gold is connected to the sun, and is a very positive and forceful energy that is good when dealing with very chaotic or disruptive forces. This colour is associated with the yang principle on a spiritual level.

The following exercise can be used to increase the strength of your natural auric protection.

EXERCISE

Protection

(ten minutes)

***Aim**: To strengthen your natural auric protection.*

- Find a place where you can sit undisturbed.
- Choose a colour, either white, blue or gold.
- Carry out the **inner light exercise** from Chapter 3.
- Close your eyes and imagine or sense that you are creating a bubble of light composed of your chosen colour extending to about 2ft around you. Make sure that this light is above your head as well as under your feet.

- Practise sensing or imagining this light expanding and contracting until you feel that you have found the most comfortable distance.
- Practise sensing or imagining this light alternating between being stationary and spinning like a top.
- Open your eyes and sense that this protection is still around you.
- When you have tried this out with one colour, try another.
- Assess which colour you feel most comfortable with and note down any other feelings or sensations.

Ideally a protection exercise should be carried out before any healing work is undertaken. It can also become a very useful addition before and after meditation exercises. I always spend a few moments each day, in the morning when I get up and just before going to bed, in balancing and protecting my aura.

With practice, and by reducing the time spent relaxing, it can become an almost instantaneous response that can be called upon in any emergency situations. Practice is important. You can soon learn to carry out this exercise with your eyes open. Try doing it when you have a few moments to yourself, such as travelling on the train to work. The more that you do this the stronger your aura becomes, for each attempt has an accumulative effect.

Protecting yourself in this way does not stop you being aware of or cutting yourself off from life's experiences, no more than we can cut ourselves off from experiencing different weather conditions. What it does is provide you with the necessary equipment to explore these different energies in a balanced way; to experience different energies without being overwhelmed by them.

Symbols and Protection

Symbols have been used since ancient times for protection. They can either be in amulet form, such as a necklace, ring or bracelet, or they can be imaged as part of your auric field. Each symbol carries a slightly different quality of feeling and potency. To begin with pick out the symbols that attract you the most from those suggested in this chapter. You can experiment with them to test your response. These symbols work on a subtle level and the conscious mind is not always the best judge. A person could, for example, perceive no intellectual association with, say, the caduceus, but in psychically sensing or 'tuning into' this symbol they could feel a very strong affinity with it. The same is true of the colours. You might not like blue as a colour around your house, or wearing it as part of your clothes, but it could be the most appropriate protective colour in your aura. Some more protective symbols include the pentangle, Star of David, the Algiz Rune, the Eye of Horus, a shield and a mirror.

Protecting Other Things and Other People

Once the principles of protection have been mastered they can be applied with equal success to all sorts of situations and to other people who might need some extra assistance. In these cases, instead of surrounding yourself with a colour or symbol, encompass the object or person.

Some examples of place or people where you can apply a protection are:

- to your home;
- to your car;
- to your family members;

Some Protective Symbols

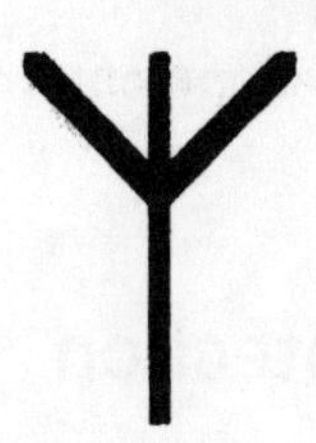

Algiz Rune

Pentangle

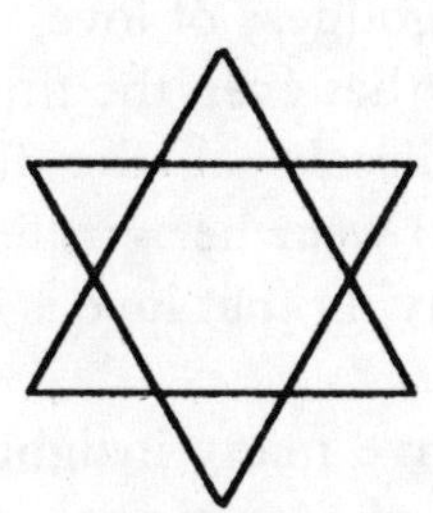

Star of David

Eye of Horus

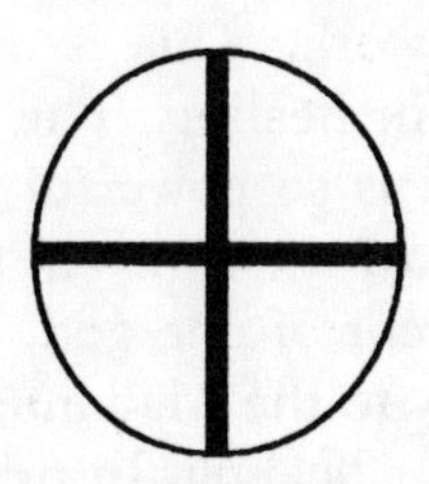

Cross within a Circle

Ankh

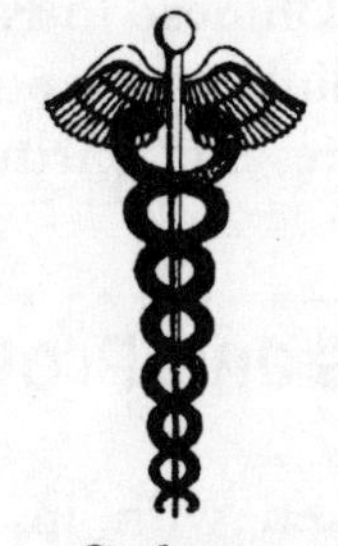

Caduceus

- to your workplace;
- to your meditation room or space;
- around any healing or psychic development group;
- to a project.

Mythology and Protection

Stories in mythology and literature abound with accounts of gods and goddesses coming to the aid of the heroes. In the Greek myths, Aphrodite, the goddess of love, owned a magic girdle. The stories tell us that even the thunderbolts of Zeus would fall harmlessly at the feet of whomever Aphrodite permitted to wear her girdle. This was the Ancient Greeks' way of saying that love is one of the greatest protectors.

Exploring ancient myths can give many insights into different types of protection and the particular god or goddess to invoke or pray to for assistance. These beings represent archetypal energies that we can call upon equally to assist in our healing work. This is another variation on the use of symbols in healing. The desire within to make these connections is so powerful that it will often override the prejudices of the time. In theory Christianity is based on the concept of one god, but in practice many Christians will pray to the Madonna or to one of the saints for intercession or healing. In principle this is little different from the Ancient Egyptians praying to Isis or the Ancient Chinese to Kwan-Yin, the goddess of mercy. Each will link us through to a very similar energy source that represents spiritual love in the cosmos.

Animals and Protection

Animals can be worked with in two ways: first in a symbolic sense and secondly as a working partnership.

Animals are very sensitive to different energies and will immediately detect imbalances or disturbances. Some people build up a practical working association with animals in their healing work. They will always have them present in the room when carrying out healing or some other psychic activity. Animals' ability to sense and perceive subtle energies is generally far in excess of our own. Animals communicate through telepathic mental images which, with practice, we can learn to interpret. If you live on your own and have no friend or colleague with whom you can work, then an animal companion could prove a more than adequate substitute. Developing working associations with animals can be a very fruitful experience. Cats and dogs are the easiest to work with, because they have had a long association with human beings, but in theory any animal can be partnered in this way.

You can also work with animals on a imagery level. Shamanistic tradition talks about power animals that will come and work with you in your healing and meditative work. At a psychological level these animals could be seen to represent aspects of your own nature. For example, if you sensed a lion was walking beside you it would be because you carry the inner strength that we normally associate with lions. However, in my own experience these power animals have an independence about them that suggests they are not just aspects of ourselves. These animal forms could also be the spirits of real animals that have chosen to work with us at a subtle level. Seen in another way it is a variation on those healers who feel the presence of different spirit guides who help them in their work. Many healers believe that their work attracts the support of beings from the spiritual realm, but you do not have to aware of these other dimensions to be a good healer. If you do sense these presences try to build a connection with them as they can be very helpful in dealing with certain types of conditions.

If I am involved in healing very disturbed energies in places or within people I always connect to a lioness who immediately conveys to me through her imaged actions what is happening. If she sits quietly by my feet then I know all is well. If she starts to get up and prowl around then I know I need to be on my guard. With practice it is not too difficult to sense or 'see', or be aware of these animal presences.

Psychic Self-Defence

There can be occasions where individuals try to use their psychic or mental Ch'i to gain a hold over others. This is against cosmic law and will eventually rebound upon the perpetrator: 'As ye sow, so shall ye reap'. But in the mean time they can cause individuals considerable suffering. If you suspect that this is happening either to you or someone who has asked for your help then you will need to strengthen your protections. In such cases working within a group structure is much the safest approach. As has already been stated energy will flow from the strongest to the weakest point. There is a principle within the cosmos that indicates that we will only experience that which we can tackle ourselves. So, if you do not go out looking for trouble you will only attract to you those circumstances that are conducive to your level of experience. However, in some cases this can mean learning to tackle quite disturbed or chaotic energies. I prefer to call these energies disturbed rather than using the term evil, but the terminology makes little difference in practice. Some energies can be very difficult to tackle and need to be approached with considerable caution. When carrying out any healing that involves the clearing of energies of places or healing what are loosely referred to as possession cases you should not under any circumstances work alone. If you are drawn to this type of healing work you should only do so under strict instruction from a competent teacher and preferably also within the confines of a group structure where several colleagues can work together. When carrying out such work within a group always allocate some members to be solely responsible for the protection. This is a safety-first procedure which if followed will ensure that the exploration into these realms can be carried out with enjoyment and fulfilment. You will find further details of this in Chapters 11 and 12.

There is another aspect of this type of phenomenon that can loosely be called 'psychic vampirism'. This conjures up all sorts of lurid pictures but in practice it often happens quite naturally, when someone is very low on energy. If they find it difficult to recharge themselves properly when asleep they might unconsciously leech Ch'i out of others around them in their daily life. This was referred to in Chapter 1.

The story of a well-known healer who was also a vicar adds a further dimension to this form of experience. One particular patient used to visit the healer on a regular basis and seemed to gain much help from the contact, until one day he missed his appointment. For many months he never got back in touch, but in the mean time the healer, for no apparent reason and at all sorts of odd times, would suddenly feel totally drained of energy. He could not understand what was happening and thought he must have some form of illness. Eventually the healer accidentally bumped into his patient again and, asking how he fared, was met with a very sheepish expression. The patient confessed that he had been very sorry to have missed the appointment which was caused by some unforeseen circumstances. Feeling so desperate for healing he confessed to having 'tuned into' the healer and had then felt an immediate beneficial response. The patient then concluded from this that perhaps it was not necessary actually to 'see' the particular healer as he was a busy person. Instead, whenever he needed help he just 'tuned in' and felt healing energy coming to him from the healer. The vicar felt the penny drop as he realised why he had suddenly felt so tired at all sorts of different times.

Ch'i Depletion

Many individuals I have met have had similar experiences. In one particular case it was an aged mother who was drawing upon the Ch'i of her daughter, in another a sick relative and in another again a close friend. In all these cases there was a deep cry of help from the suffering individual. Some professionals like teachers, nurses, counsellors or therapists can be prone to this type of problem.

There are two possible solutions to this. The first is to affirm quite strongly within that your Ch'i will never be drained in this way. Then put a strong protection around yourself to prevent this scenario happening. You can build in the thought that this protection will immediately come into force if anyone tries to tap into your energy. Alternatively, you can adopt the opposite approach by saying that anyone can tap into your Ch'i, but as soon as this happens they are immediately connected through you to your normal source of healing Ch'i. In other words, if you normally think of the sun as your source of healing energy and someone tries to tap into you, then that link immediately opens up. Effectively then, they will draw from your healing Ch'i and not from your personal Ch'i. As with healing you will not then be drained of energy (see Chapter 5 for more on this). I tend to favour this latter approach but it needs to be an individual decision.

If ever you suddenly feel drained of energy, depleted of Ch'i, then link to your source of healing power and feel it flowing into you. You will be surprised how effective and immediate this can be.

Do Protections Work?

It is always very difficult to evaluate the potency of psychic protections except through individual experiences. I have known people who have stepped out unscathed from cars that have been written off in major accidents, who have disturbed burglars before their house was ransacked, who have found they have been able to cope with life when before they felt they were continually battered by difficult situations and different vibrational energies. In all these cases the individuals felt that psychic protection had helped them.

Perhaps the most dramatic story that came back to me after one of the healing courses that I ran in the mid 1970s was from an Australian woman who owned a ranch. Shortly after she had returned home a serious bush fire broke out in her area and stared to move swiftly towards her property. Fearing she might lose everything she first brought all the stock in close to the building then remembered about protection. In her mind she built a protection right around her establishment. The fire moved right up to the edge of where she had visualised the protection. Then, for no apparent reason, it split and went either side around the edge of her ring. Eventually it petered out and everything inside was completely unscathed.

The proof of the pudding must lie in the eating. Long experience has taught me the value of using protections. However, I also know of some psychics who never bother with this aspect of work. Perhaps they are like the smoker on 60 cigarettes a day who lives to the ripe old age of 90. You may be the lucky one. Whether or not you decide to put on your 'psychic' seat belt has to be an individual choice, but my strong advice would be to make a habit of always using protections when carrying out any healing or psychic work.

The following exercise can be used to supplement those already given, and to incorporate the use of animal and other symbolism.

EXERCISE

Additional Protection

(five to ten minutes)

***Aim**: This exercise will allow you to draw upon the creativity of your own mind to strengthen your auric protection. It is rather like trying on different clothes to see which suit.*

- Repeat the previous exercise but this time ask within for a colour to represent protection.
- Now imagine an animal that symbolises protection for you. Where would you place the animal in relationship to yourself?
- Next visualise a flower that symbolises protection. Where does this flower rest in relation to your body?
- Visualise an item of clothing that represents protection and feel yourself wearing this clothing. When would you most need to wear it?

- Finally, slowly bring yourself back to full waking consciousness.
- Note down your response to the symbols and any associations at a mental or emotional level. Which did you feel comfortable with and which did you not.

Your Subtle Energy Fields

To maintain your centre is to endure.
(TAO 33)

The simplest way to understand the subtle energy fields of the body is to return to the analogy of our piano keyboard. As we have seen, each octave on the keyboard can be seen as an octave of Ch'i at finer and finer levels of frequency. Scientific instruments can at present only measure those frequencies that are very close to the physical world. Perhaps in time scientists will be able to measure emotional and mental energy at its pure energetic level, but at present they cannot. In consequence the majority of scientists deny these other levels of experience. Esoteric schools have given names to these aspects of our being and many healers will have come across these terms.

In essence the easiest way to describe these energy fields is to relate them to your everyday experiences. For example, your emotions are energies that both weave within the body as well as project out from you. If someone displays a strong emotion sensitive people will immediately feel this when they are in their vicinity. Many have had the experience of a boss or partner who is upset or angry and without saying anything the feeling is immediately communicated. The researches of Professor

Jahn, mentioned in Chapter 1, on psycho-kinetic effects, has shown that even at great distances thoughts affect objects and they will certainly affect other people. In its simplest form you could therefore be said to have a physical energy field, an emotional energy field, a mental energy field and a spiritual energy field, each being a higher octave of the preceding energy field. Psychics and esotericists, however, have often further subdivided this array.

According to many traditions the next octave to the physical body is the etheric body. This is said to be an exact counterpart to the physical shell, and carries the resonant energies between the physical body and the emotions. The emotional body is known as the astral body, which is usually divided into a lower astral and higher astral level. The former carries all the basic instincts, the fight/flight responses, while the latter responds to emotions of love, peace, happiness etc. We then move on to the lower mental body that is responsible for rational or logical thought, and the higher mental body that links to abstract or conceptual thought. Above the mental body comes the intuitive body and finally in some schools what is referred to as the Buddhic or spiritual body. This links to the higher spiritual aspect of our consciousness.

The above terms have their place in the sense that they imply there are resonant energy fields that correspond to each of these bodies. This can take us out of just seeing emotions as an aspect of the physical body and thoughts an aspect of the brain. As terms they can create a jargon that for some is offputting. It is all a question of individual choice.

While speaking of these bodies as though they are layers it should be appreciated that they all interpenetrate. Just as an orchestra playing a symphony will sound a complete range of notes across the audible spectrum, so also at any moment you can express thoughts, feelings and physical sensations, and the wisdom of your spiritual self.

Healing Ch'i will flow into these energy fields and naturally seek those aspects that need harmonising. When sending healing to someone else the sensitive healer can learn to detect which aspect of the energy field is out of balance and focus their healing accordingly. This will be dealt with fully in Chapter 5. Some individuals can 'see' the colours of these fields and will use this as a method of diagnosis. It should be remembered that this is an individual perception and two psychics 'tuning into' the same individual might see very different colours. What is important is how they interpret those colours and what they need to do to bring balance to the whole self. This form of diagnosis will be discussed fully in Chapter 8.

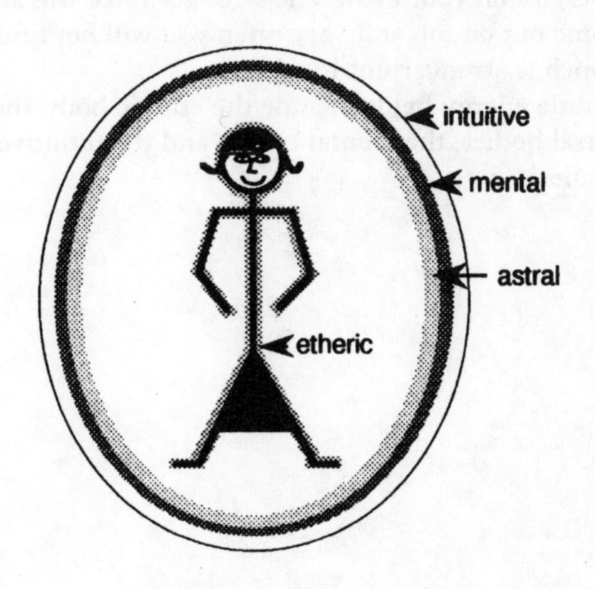

Ch'i Fields

Summary

- Protection is a natural part of human experience, and needs to be applied at all levels of healing and meditative work.
- Your basic protection at an energetic level is the 'aura'.
- Developing healing and psychic gifts will increase sensitivity to other subtle energies, potentially making you susceptible to disturbances.
- White, blue and gold are the three colours traditionally associated with protection.
- Protection can be applied to many things apart from yourself.
- Be very wary of trying to tackle chaotic or disruptive energies on your own. The stronger force will always come out on top and very often you will not find out which is stronger until you start.
- Subtle energy fields include the etheric body, the astral bodies, the mental bodies and the intuitive bodies.

CHAPTER 5

Healing Techniques

Through loving service
You will attain fulfillment.

(TAO 7)

Often the easiest way to experience healing Ch'i is by learning how to direct if for the benefit of others. The very act of giving healing will help you balance aspects of yourself. There is always a two-way connection

Healing is a natural gift we all possess to a greater or lesser degree, and like all gifts it can be developed with practice and patience. It is a gift that can be used in all sorts of situations and can be a valuable asset for all of us. There are many circumstances such as accidents or illnesses of friends or members of the family where healing energy can speed recovery. It is also very effective in helping maintain a balance within young children and adolescents. I normally send out a thought of balancing healing Ch'i every day to my children which I feel helps them greatly in their development. This need only take a few minutes and they do not have to be present or even aware of what is being carried out. The positive effect of this is very noticeable in their lives.

There are many professions, such as nursing,

counselling, teaching and all types of complementary therapies, where the understanding and use of the healing Ch'i can be a powerful adjunct to one's work. The single most important aspect is a desire to help others and, second to that, a belief that healing energies can flow through you. It used to be known as faith healing, which is perhaps a fair description except it is the healer who needs to have the faith not the patient. As we saw in the Byrd studies in the introduction the patient's beliefs have no direct impact upon the efficacy of the healing.

Healing Hands

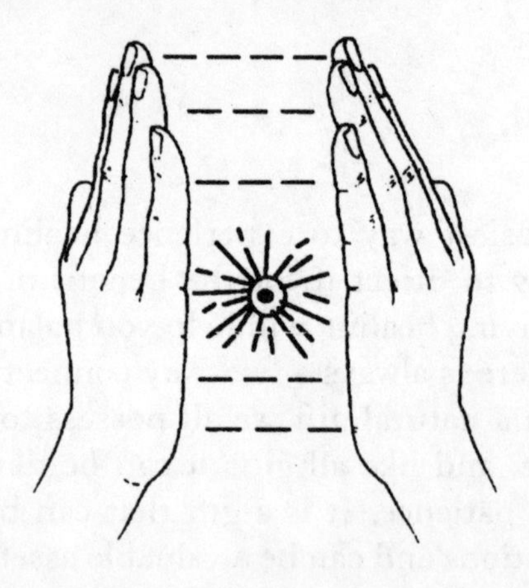

It is through our hands that we can generate some of the most powerful Ch'i energies. When sending healing to someone else imagine that the healing Ch'i is flowing from your source of healing, through your body and out from your hands towards the patient. Working with your hands in this way gives a much broader range of energies than just focusing your energy through your mind. One exercise that healers often do is rub their hands together to stimulate the Ch'i. Try this for yourself and then hold your hands in the position above, and try and sense the Ch'i flowing between them. You could further add to this by imagining that you are holding a ball of light between your hands.

Some people feel uncomfortable about the use of the word 'healer' in that it gives a sense of separateness and superiority over those who will be receiving the healing. This is a quite understandable response. The use of the word 'healer' in this book implies only 'one who is sending out or proposing to send healing energies to another'. It does not suggest any exalted status or professional expertise.

Ways to Heal

There is no one way to heal or send out Ch'i, indeed there could be said to be as many ways as there are healers. Discover the method that suits you best and work with that, allowing it to develop in the most natural way that you can. In its broadest sense it could be said that all forms of human interaction that seek to establish harmony and balance could be regarded as healing disciplines. However, many therapeutic approaches do not recognise the importance of the link between the spiritual self and body, so working on this aspect is perhaps one of the most valuable contributions that healers can make. Of all systems of treatment it is the only one that can work directly on the soul/mind connection. All systems of therapy have their places and areas of greatest effectiveness, so all are important.

Applied healing energies have helped all manner of conditions and the miraculous cures of Christ are but examples of what can be achieved. Healing energy can be directed to patients at a distance often referred to as 'absent healing' or to patients present with you. It makes little difference whether the person is sitting in front of you or on the other side of the globe. Ch'i can also be directed to help heal life situations, such as can be found in relationships.

All healing should be an offering to assist another

individual to find balance within. At no time should you ever try and impose your will over others. Of all the gifts that we possess probably the greatest is our gift of free will and this should be respected at all times. You need to appreciate also that there are those individuals who at a deep spiritual level choose to suffer the conditions that they are experiencing. With these people you should be aware of the difference between the wishes of their spiritual self and the dictates of their conscious 'ego' mind. In my experience the spiritual self very rarely rejects healing completely, as long as it is sent in the right way.

For example, a person may be suffering a chronic condition, and seek the aid of both orthodox and complementary treatment to relieve this problem. If their soul wishes to experience this type of illness, for whatever reason, no treatment will provide an effective cure. What healing can do in such a case is help the spiritual self assess its experience. This will help it derive the greatest benefit from what it has chosen to undergo. In a world where death is generally regarded as a form of failure, this type of thinking can seem bizarre. In reality we need to see life as a continuum, where the spiritual essence goes on experiencing eternally. If you can accept this fact, the shedding of the physical body at death is then of minor significance.

Reaching a level of healing ability where you can be sure of the wishes of the spiritual self of the person that you are working with, requires considerable understanding. If you approach your healing from the point of view that you are balancing the whole person, body, emotions, mind and spirit, you will get over this problem. A useful catch-all phrase that many healers use is to affirm within **'Thy Will be done'**. This covers both the inner spiritual will of the client, as well as the more orthodox belief in the 'Will of God'. The spiritual self within the person will determine how best to use the quality of energy you have to offer. If you then sense the need to direct your energies to the specific problem, as part of the healing treatment, do so knowing that you have set up the right safeguards.

You can work alone or with others. However, in embarking upon an exploration of your healing energies it can be very helpful to work with others who are already treading the path. In this way you can learn from their wide experience and gain confidence in your ability to help others. If you choose to work on your own this book will give you the necessary tools to do so.

Localised or General Healing?

Interestingly, repeated studies carried out at Spindthrift in USA also suggest that healing is much less effective when it is only localised. In other words if a person comes to see you with, say, a heart condition and the healing is directed specifically to that organ, then you will be between two to four times less successful than if you just sent healing to the whole person. You need to focus on bringing balance to the totality of the individual, whatever you sense that to be.

You also need to learn to trust that the higher aspect of yourself will forward the correct energies to help the individual to whom you are sending healing. In one sense all that is necessary is to open up to the healing energy and just let it flow through you, trusting in its efficacy. However, one of the reasons for incarnation into a physical body is to learn to ground and earth the spiritual impulses within. Because of this it is helpful to try to understand what is channelling through you so that eventually you will reach a point where the conscious mind and your spiritual self become fused as one. You will then know, in a conscious way, why you are drawing upon particular energies and what it is that you are doing.

This is a very exciting moment when it occurs.

In a conversation I had with psychologist Lawrence LeShan, famous for his book *Clairvoyant Reality* and his work with cancer patients, we started to discuss the role of healers. He felt that most healers learnt a particular method of healing within the first few months of coming into the discipline and then stayed with that. His big plea was that we should continually strive to push out the boundaries of our healing ability. One of the reasons, he went on to say, for physicists making such huge strides in the area of quantum physics was because **'they continually challenged their assumptions'**. If healers would only do the same, he felt, we would make enormous leaps in understanding the subtle nature of reality, thus making us much better healers. This is a sentiment with which I wholeheartedly agree, so I would strongly encourage all prospective healers to explore their gift freely and expansively, trying to understand how they can be more effective.

Sources of Healing Energy

Once you have determined that you wish to send healing to another person the next most important move is to understand the origin of your energy. There are two primary sources that we can draw upon. We can either use our own energies or we can connect into reservoirs of energy outside of ourself and thus become a channel for that energy.

When healers first embark upon giving healing there is often a tendency to draw upon their own energies. The drawback here is that you will very quickly end up depleting your system and feeling totally drained yourself. This is not a good state to be in, particularly as a healer. The late Max Cade carried out some studies on healers in the mid 1970s. His findings suggested that those healers who used only their own energy could give treatment to three or four people at the most before being totally exhausted. If they continued after that point a reversal took place and they would then start to draw Ch'i back out of the patient. Obviously this is not good for the patients. However, those healers who saw themselves as a channel for healing energies could go on treating many patients with little impairment of their abilities. The key then is to learn to act as a channel for healing energies and not to draw upon your reserves.

Try to keep it simple to begin with. Some ideas on sources of Ch'i have already been given in Chapter 1, but in practice the list is endless. Each source of Ch'i will give a slightly different flavour of energy, so to begin with it is better to use the broadest, most general source that you feel comfortable with, as this will give you the best results. If you are religious, you could link with God, in whatever way you understand that force to be. For those who find difficulty with this concept, try thinking of the sun. The energy from the sun covers many spectrums and at a basic level is the source of light and life within this solar system. There is no restriction on what can be used, indeed one healer I know imagines that they are connecting themselves to the electricity circuit for their energy – and it works! Alternative sources of Ch'i include: religious teachers and saints (Christ, Buddha, Mohammed, Akhenaten, St Christopher etc.); gods and goddesses from the different pantheons (Isis, Kwan Yin, Ganesh, Odin, Athene etc.); angels and archangels (Michael, Uriel, Raphael, Gabriel etc.); the natural world (trees, flowers, mountains, rivers etc.); spirit beings from the four elements (earth, air, fire and water); human spirit beings (White Eagle, Red Cloud, Silver Birch, Chan etc); power animals (wolf, bear, lion, eagle etc.); planetary bodies (Venus, Mercury, Jupiter etc.); stellar bodies (Sun, Sirius, Aldebran, Arcturus etc.); musical sounds and notes; colours of the spectrum; sacred places (Lourdes,

Great Pyramid, Avebury, Chartres Cathedral etc.); symbols (caduceus, golden chalice, etc.); and other people who have given consent for their energy to be used.

With practice the adventurous healer can learn to channel a wider and wider range of frequencies. For example someone who is feeling very agitated or hyperactive would need a quality of energy that conveys a feeling of peace and calm. Someone feeling very depressed or lethargic might need a more enlivening quality of Ch'i to help shift them into a more positive outlook. One of the best ways you can learn to work with these different qualities is by using colour rays and symbols, and these will be discussed more fully in Chapter 6.

There appears to be no set attitude of mind that healers have to adopt to be effective in their treatment. I have witnessed healers carrying on conversations with their clients, sometimes on subjects totally divorced from the particular complaint. Other healers like to maintain quiet while they are healing. There is a suggested technique given in this book for linking to the deeper layers of yourself but ultimately you need to develop your own system. Nor is there any set time limit for giving healing. The general rule seems to be to give the healing for as long as you feel that it is necessary. The quickest healer I ever witnessed was a Russian parapsychologist named Barbara Ivanova, who would direct her healing energies for as little as 15 to 30 seconds. Barbara worked on the principle that she was putting energy into the body and experience had taught her that she could focus a large amount of energy very quickly. Too much energy being sent into the body can make a person feel very uncomfortable, hence her time restriction. Conversely I have seen healers giving healing for as long as an hour. I will give healing for as long as I can hold my attention on what I am doing. This lasts somewhere between five and ten minutes. As soon as my mind begins to wander I draw the healing to a close.

The Application of Healing Energy

We have seen how healing energy can operate in three different ways. It can be used to:

- put Ch'i into the system;
- balance what is already there;
- remove unwanted Ch'i.

Many healers feel that they are not being successful unless they are pumping a lot of energy into their patient. This may not always be necessary. If we go back to our piano analogy, problems occur when the piano gets out of tune. This causes blockages in the flow of energy and disharmony in the sound of the piano. Some notes may only be slightly off pitch, and can very easily and gently be brought back into harmony by adjusting the tone of the notes. Alternatively, some part of the piano could have become damaged from being mistreated and in these cases repairs need to be carried out requiring a lot of energy. Finally dirt and grime could have become encrusted on to the strings, causing them to sound off key. In these cases the dirt and grime needs to be removed before the piano comes back into tune. In a similar way you can learn to use the power of your mind to balance the energies of your patient, remove energies that should not be there or put energy into the system to repair damage.

Balancing energies generally requires very little effort. Surrounding a person in a thought of peace or love will have that effect. If unwanted energies become caught up within a person these will need to be drawn off to bring about the healing. At a physical level, viral or bacteriological infections are a form of inappropriate energy where a type of invasion has taken place. Invasive energies can occur at every level, as can be seen in crowd hysteria, where the power of the emotion becomes so strong that individuals can be sucked in, causing behavioural activities at odds with their more rational instincts. Sometimes individuals feel they have picked up some disturbed force within their energy fields. Clearing or cleansing these energies is a very important part of the healing process. Finally, there are those situations, when directing positive Ch'i, considerable power may be needed to repair damage that has occurred at either a physical, emotional, mental or spiritual level. The principle objective of all healers should be 'How can I help this person find balance and harmony within?'

We are all unique individuals, so the healing energy that you attract will reflect your own energy balances. Over time some healers find that they start to specialise, in the sense that they seem to get better results with certain types of conditions. This is a natural progressive step and while it is important to be open to treating all levels and types of conditions, life may draw more specific types of cases to you. This interconnecting element within the universe is very magical. When you are ready for something to happen it will happen.

The process of giving healing to another will help balance your own energies. It is always a two-way process. This can sometimes take the form of highlighting the part of yourself that requires attention. It is therefore very important to be open to receiving help yourself, particularly if some part of your life gets seriously out of balance. Never be too proud to ask for help and healing for yourself.

Physical problems are very often the end result of imbalances at other levels. As long as these are also corrected, which generally means a shift in perspective within the individual, the physical symptoms will not return. If the underlying causes are not dealt with, however, there will always be a return of the symptoms. This is why some individuals receive amazing temporary relief from a condition after seeing a healer or at a charismatic healing service only for the condition to return again a few months later.

Can I Harm Another by Giving Healing?

A question that many novice healers often ask is 'Can I do any harm by giving healing?' The answer to this is both yes and no. We need to accept the responsibility for the Ch'i that we are wielding. If in arrogance you determine that you are going to shift another's energy, to 'make them well', you could be causing all sorts of problems. If, on the other hand, you offer healing Ch'i with love to another to help them find balance and wholeness, no harm will ever result. It is just a question of intention and attitude. Remember, it is wrong to inflict your will over another.

Attitudes in healing are therefore very important. There will always be a subtle connection between healer and patient that is not obvious on the surface. Healers have as much to learn and gain from their patients as they have from us. I sometimes reflect when giving healing to another, **'What is the part in me that I am healing within this individual?'** The very act of healing will also spark off inner development. As a healer you need to be sensitive to balancing your own energies and maintaining your own sense of poise.

Healing Procedure

In learning to develop your healing techniques it is perhaps easier to start by sending distant healing. This allows you to go at your own speed without feeling self-conscious. The procedural steps suggested below apply to both direct contact healing as well as distant healing.

Suggested Healing Procedure

1. Attune to your spiritual self or inner light.
2. Attune to the subject and their spiritual self.
3. Link to your source of healing energy, e.g. Christ, Godhead, sun, cosmos, golden chalice, the earth.
4. Direct your thoughts to balance the whole of the energy field of the subject.
5. Send healing to the specific parts, e.g. an arthritic knee.
6. Balance the whole person again.
7. De-link from your source of energy and from the subject.
8. Sense yourself balanced within and close down.

Let us look at these stages in a little more detail.

1. When attuning within, you can follow the exercise 'Connecting to Your Inner Light', given in Chapter 3. With practice this can be speeded up so that it takes but a few moments. It provides a space for sensing the connection to the deepest part of your self.
2. When you attune to the subject all that is necessary is to have the thought that you are connecting to the highest part of their being, rather than to their outer personality. In this way you will open up the connection to their spiritual self. Remember to acknowledge that it is an offering of healing that you are giving them, not an imposition.
3. To link to your source of healing energy visualise or sense that a connection is being made and draw that energy through you. For example, if you wished to use the sun as a source of Ch'i, you could imagine that a golden beam of sunlight was entering through the top of your head and being channelled to the subject.
4. The simplest way to balance the energies of the whole person is to see them surrounded in a sphere of light, or energy field, that is connecting to all aspects of their

Healing Treatment

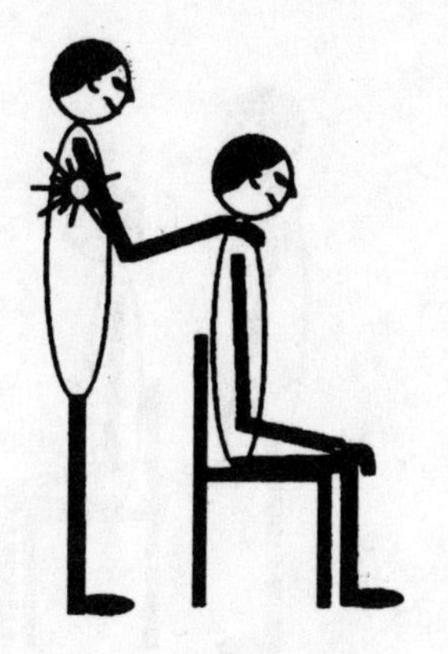

Stage 1
Attune within

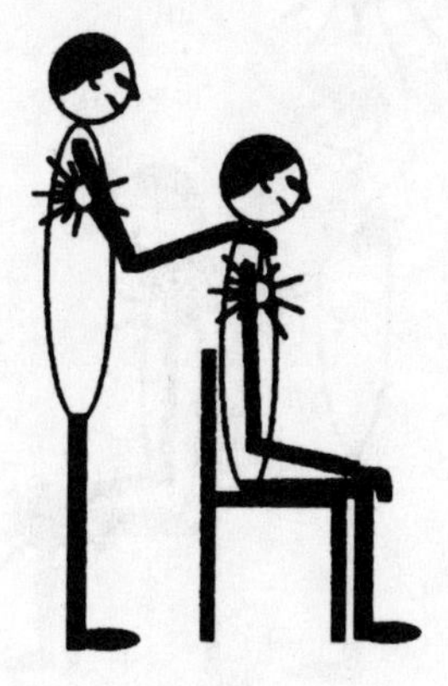

Stage 2
Attune to subject

Stage 3
Connect to healing Ch'i

Stage 4 and 6
Healing to whole being

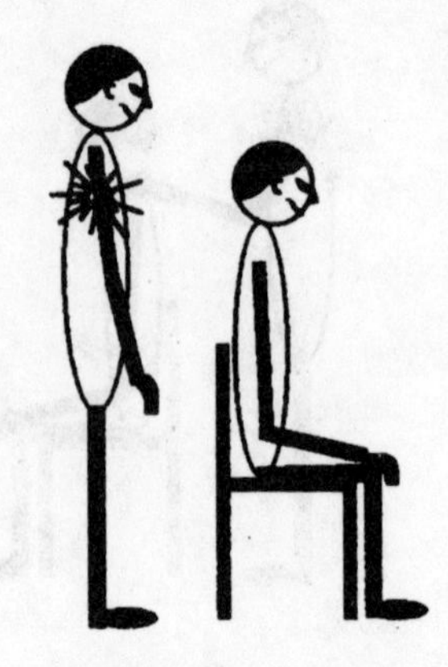

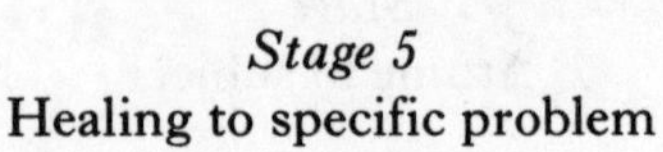

Stage 5
Healing to specific problem

Stage 6 and 7
Disconnect and close down

being: body, emotions, mind and spirit. You can also hold the thought that they are whole and balanced within themselves.

5. When sending the healing to the specific part, the easiest way is to hold your hands close to or over the affected area. Sense the energy coming through your hands and correcting the imbalances, whatever they might be, of the affected part. Details of different colour rays that you can use are given in the next chapter. When sending distant healing you will need to imagine or visualise that an energy beam of light is focusing through to the location of the problem. For example, if a subject suffers from arthritic knees, having first sent healing to the whole person you could imagine that the healing energy is freeing up the affected joints.

   This is also a stage when you can allow your imagination full rein. With arthritic joints one healer I know would visualise a large oil can, holding a golden liquid, which they would then squirt liberally into any affected joints. Remember also that physical conditions will in general also have an emotional or mental element. Healing can also be sent to these aspects of the self.

6. Repeat step 4, sensing that all aspects are being balanced within the individual. Normally I will also send an extra thought to strengthening the subject's aura at this stage.
7. It is important that you disconnect from the subject at this stage, and sense that the energy link between you is no longer flowing. If you do not do this you will continue to feel yourself being drawn upon by the subject. It is also important to disconnect from the source of the healing energy. When you initially connect to your source, your higher mind will plug you into a particular aspect of energy that is right for the subject, but may not be right for you. Let us suppose that your subject metaphorically needs a 'green' energy which you channel to them during the healing session. If you do not disconnect from that source, the 'green' energy will continue to flow into you. However it may be that whilst this energy is good for the subject, it is not helpful to yourself and could lead to imbalances occurring. This is why we need to disconnect from our healing sources at the end of each session.
8. Finally spend a few moments sensing the balance of energy within yourself, and try and feel that every part of you is whole and integrated.

Distant Healing

The simplest way to send distant healing to a person is to imagine or sense that they are sitting in front of you. You do **not** have to visualise them in great detail for the healing to work. Just having the feeling that they are there is enough. When you have finished, sense or imagine that you are lifting them up into the light, and then you are free to go on to the next case.

Direct Healing

When you are giving direct healing to a person it is preferable to have them either sitting in a straight chair, or lying on the floor or couch. As the 'healer' you need to be in a position that is comfortable for you. If possible place your hands on their shoulders as a preliminary to starting the healing. This may not always be possible, if say, you were giving healing to someone in a hospital bed. However, touch is very important and creates an initial bond, and in the latter case holding a person's hand could be just as effective. Thereafter you can either use physical contact in directing your healing energies or work with your hands set at between 12 to 18 in from the client. Many healers feel self-conscious when they begin, particularly if not using physical contact. With practice this can cease to be a problem. You will sense the healing energy flowing through your hands quite naturally and it can then be directed as appropriate. When you have finished it is always good to send out a thought of thanks for help that you have received.

Given below is a simple healing exercise that you can safely use to start you on the path of healing. Think of someone who needs help or healing. It could be a friend or member of your family, or indeed an animal. Until you are more practised it is better to choose individuals who are not facing very severe problems.

EXERCISE

Distant Healing

(fifteen minutes)

Aim: *To send healing to another person.*

Sit in one of the positions suggested in the **body awareness exercise**. Close your eyes for a few moments focus on your breathing. Feel it is gentle and relaxed. Imagine or sense that there is a tiny flame of light within that represents your inner spiritual self. Try and either sense or 'see' where you locate this within, and feel yourself connecting to it. Then carry out the following exercise.

- Imagine or sense that the person that you are going to send healing to is sitting in front of you.
- Sense that you are connecting to their spiritual self. To make this more real you could imagine that you are linking the light within you to the light within them by means of a golden thread. Affirm within the words, 'Thy Will be done'.
- Connect to your source of healing energy and feel it flowing down through the top of your head, through your hands to the person.
- Sense or hold the thought in your mind that this energy is balancing the whole person. To make this more real you could imagine a pair of scales superimposed over the person. Hold the thought until you sense the scales are balanced.
- Allow your imagination to prompt you to any other aspect that needs healing in a specific way. For example, if you know that they have a damaged ankle, focus the healing energy there.

- Return back to sending healing once more to the whole person, but this time imagine also that they are surrounded in a bubble of light.
- Disconnect the golden light that you held between you, and disconnect also from the source of energy that is flowing through you.
- Sit for a moment, sensing that you are balancing your own energies before opening your eyes.

Write down your experiences. Keeping up a journal can be a helpful device for monitoring your progress. Some healers also like to wash their hands after each case and this too can be a useful discipline, symbolising the de-linking of energy from the patient.

Once you have gained the confidence to use your mind to channel Ch'i energy to benefit another look for all the experiences in your life where it might be relevant and helpful. You can send healing to friends, members of your family, pets, plants and others that you know are sick, and in Chapter 10 we will look at how healing can be sent to world situations. There is no shortage of applications for this energy, and on a progressive level it will deepen your understanding and insight and bring forward a sense of purpose, knowing that you can do something positive to contribute to the well-being of others.

When Not to Give Healing

Before completing this chapter a few words need to be said on when not to give healing. Apart from those cases requiring specialist training, healing can always be given on the proviso that you the healer are in a reasonably healthy state. Clearly this is more difficult when healers rely on seeing patients for their livelihood. However, there is a responsibility to the patient that over-rides this consideration. If as a healer you are feeling run-down, depressed, or suffering symptoms of a cold or flu do not attempt to give healing to someone else. In this category I would also include all individuals suffering mental illness. Allow yourself time to recover fully before re-embarking on giving healing.Those cases that require specialist training include: cancer; all severe mental illnesses such as manic-depressive psychosis and schizophrenia; individuals who feel they are 'possessed'; individuals who feel they have been 'cursed'; hauntings; individuals who have been involved in black magic practices; alcoholics and drug addicts.

Summary

- Healing is a natural gift we all possess.
- There are as many ways to heal as there are healers.
- All healing should be an offering to help another find balance and wholeness within.
- Healing works better when it is directed to the whole person rather than the specific illness.
- As healers we need to learn to channel healing energy rather than using our own energies.
- Healing can be directed to putting energy into the system, balancing what is already there or drawing energy out of the system.
- As healers you need to be mindful of maintaining a balance of your own energies.

CHAPTER 6
Using Colour And Symbol

To follow the Tao
Is to honour its principles,
To realise:
That we live in nature
But can never own it;
We can guide and serve,
But never dominate,
This is the highest wisdom.

(TAO 51)

Colours and Healing

We have already seen that healing Ch'i is not like electricity. It carries with it very many distinct flavours that healers and sensitive individuals can soon learn to detect. In this sense it is very akin to music with all its many nuances. The music of Mozart is nothing like that of the Rolling Stones and will produce a different type of response within an audience. Indeed there is a very close parallel between music and healing, with the energies of these two expressions overlapping each other. In past times music and sound were closely associated with healing, and still find expression today in chanting and the temple bells of Tibet. Describing how to work with sound and music for healing is outside the scope of this work, but if you are interested in discovering more, you will find details of books on the subject in the Bibliography. A simpler approach, that most people can use, is working with colour and symbols. Instead of just imagining Ch'i coming from your hands, you can consciously direct a specific colour ray to bring about the necessary change. With a little practice this becomes very easy and can considerably increase the effectiveness of your healing.

Colour in Your Own Energy Field

You can also use colour within your own auric energy field, depending upon what activity you wish to pursue. One healer I know always surrounds himself with a 'blue' light before giving any healing, whilst at other times of the day he uses a 'white' light for protection. Think about what colour light in your aura would be the most appropriate if, say, you were going for a job interview or to meet your bank manager? Working with Ch'i in this way can have some very beneficial effects in a non-invasive way.

To get the feel of working with colour you do not need a patient, but can practise by sending Ch'i to your garden or some other aspect of nature in your locality. Nature provides us with so much and this exercise will help you to recycle some of the love and support that we receive from the natural world.

EXERCISE

Healing Nature

(ten minutes)

Aim: *To work with colour to balance various aspects of nature.*

- Attune within, connect through a feeling of love with your garden and then link to your source of healing Ch'i.

- Direct Ch'i to the garden, thinking first of whatever colour comes to mind.
- After a few moments change to another colour and see if you can sense the difference, and also whether you are aware of your energy going to a different part of the garden.
- You can work through a spectrum of colours (red, orange, yellow, green, blue, indigo, violet and adding magenta to make eight) in this way, noting those colours that come easily to you and those that do not.
- When you have completed as much as you feel you can accomplish, disconnect and close down as for other healing exercises.

We all have our own natural energy frequencies that make it easier to work with some colours than others, in the same way that we each prefer certain types of music. With a little practice you will get the feel of the different qualities of energy and the sense that you can incorporate them into your healing of others.

Colour Rays

A number of colour rays are given below. These have been tried and tested in my own healing and training development. It is not an exclusive list and different schools may suggest alternative correlations. It should be appreciated that the mind acts rather like a computer. If we programme it with certain ideas it will act accordingly and using colour rays helps us become more conscious and interactive in the healing process. It should be looked upon as the first step rather than as an end in itself.

- **White ray** is a protective and recharging ray. Although white contains all colours it has a distinctive flavour of its own. It should be used in cases where a person feels very tired or depleted of energy. Energy depletions of this type will be focused either in the body if they are physically tired or in the mind if they are mentally run down. In the former case the white ray should be directed to the area of the solar plexus and in the latter to the crown of the head. It can also be used in those situations where an individual feels battered by disturbed energies around them. Sealing them in a white, auric bubble of light will greatly help. Sometimes individuals feel that they are processing a great deal of information at night, even to the extent of believing that they are working at night on a healing level. When this happens the individual can wake feeling almost as tired as when they went to sleep. If this is the case for you imagine that you are building a bubble of white light over your solar plexus just before you go to sleep.
- **Blue Ray** is the ray of cleansing. In this sense it can be used when you need to draw off energies from the body. Wounds may be purified by this ray and it is very successful in neutralising the effects of germs, dirt etc. It can also be used for washing through and harmonising the auric energy fields, and is particularly good at helping combat viral and bacteriological infections such as colds or flu. It is good practice to cleanse your subject's aura with the blue ray before finally disconnecting at the end of a healing treatment.
- **Coral or pink ray** is a warming, soothing ray and should be used for the relief of pain, headaches and in the treatment of such complaints as arthritis etc. It is also an excellent ray to use when a person is in a very agitated or distraught state emotionally or mentally. In these cases the ray should be concentrated in those areas that reflect the particular condition. With mental

agitation this should be to the region of the head and with the emotions the region of the heart or solar plexus. It is a ray that reflects the wonderful peace and calm that is seen in the statues of the Buddha.

- **Red ray** is a powerful burning ray and should be used in all cases that symbolically require drying or where there are excessive fluids. Internally it can be directed to seal gastric ulcers and externally it can be used on badly poisoned wounds or ulcerated places. It is a very physical Ch'i and is not generally suitable for emotional or mental conditions. Experience has also shown that it can cause a little discomfort when being used. This can be counteracted by also sending a dark blue/indigo ray to the surrounding area. This has a form of anaesthetic effect.
- **Indigo or dark blue ray** is predominantly the ray of the anaesthetist. It helps dull pain by causing a slight separation between the energy layers of the body. It can also be called upon in cases where an individual is close to death, where it will assist and ease the 'passing on' process.
- **Lilac or violet ray** is a building ray, stimulating new growth at a physical level. It is ideal for cases where fibres or tissues have been damaged or destroyed, such as with severe burning or cancer. The lilac ray accelerates the regeneration of new tissue and is therefore very effective in healing wounds of all types. This makes it very useful in assisting recovery from operations. It also carries a flavour of general balance and can be used to align the spirit within the body. Drawing on this ray will help if you feel that the mind of the patient is at odds with impulses coming from the soul or spiritual self.
- **Green ray** has a neutralising effect and can be very useful with individuals who feel at odds with the world. It has a blending quality that soothes the barbs that some individuals carry. It is the predominant colour of

nature and carries a similar harmonising quality. However, it is an energy that needs to be used judiciously for it can also turn a person in on themselves, encouraging introspection. This may be helpful in some cases but if there are depressive tendencies it may exaggerate this quality.

- **Yellow ray** is the ray of the mind and intellect. Its vibrant quality can stimulate mental alertness and is also very helpful in cases of despondency or gloom, helping lift depression.
- **Magenta ray** is the ray of the spiritual self and helps in all areas of transformation. It can be very useful in all cases of past-life healing.
- **Silver ray** is used in healing brain or nerve damage in that it will help new connections to be made. It needs to be used sparingly, rather as if it were a thin laser beam.
- **Gold ray** is a very powerful ray that reflects the energy of the sun in its positive or yang aspect. Physical back problems can be a reflection of energetic imbalances that run along the spine. The gold ray can be used to repair or balance these energies and therefore makes a very good adjunct for anyone who requires help from an osteopath or chiropractor. It can also help with eye conditions. It has a very protective quality that is excellent at counteracting negative or chaotic energies. It needs to be used sensitively as some individuals can find it overwhelming.

The above are the major colour rays. They will provide a basis for working on many types of conditions. Experiment with them to see if they help with your healing. The colours can be used singly or in combination, and in any treatment you may need to work using different colours in turn. If you feel drawn to using other colours try and assess the quality that lies behind them.

To use the colours in healing visualise the particular

colour coming through your hands and being directed to the area of imbalance. If you have difficulty visualising a colour, holding the thought in your mind 'I am using a white, blue or whatever ray' will suffice. Alternatively you can imagine the colour over the top of your head and feel that you are drawing the energy through you to your subject.

Nature responds very appreciatively to this type of healing, which 'green-fingered' gardeners know only too well, although with such individuals this type of healing is generally carried out intuitively rather than consciously.

Symbols and Healing

Symbols act in a very similar way to colours and can be used as a psychological aid to connecting to specific energies. Within the development of the human psyche symbolic images come closest to the language of the spiritual self. This is why dreams are predominantly pictorial rather than linguistic. Speech first occurred at a much later stage in human evolution. Writing is a symbolic representation of ideas and sounds, and pictorial languages like Chinese and Ancient Egyptian hieroglyphics contain many more layers of meaning than do phonetic alphabets like English. Symbols can take many forms as our dream world evidences, and they carry both a personal and collective meaning. In healing they can be used in three ways:

- to act as a focus for healing energy;
- to pick up information about the subject;
- to gain insights into problems and situations.

Information on how we can use symbols to gain diagnostic insight about health problems will be covered in Chapter 8. In this chapter we will concentrate on how symbols can be used to link to specific qualities of energy.

Symbols can basically be divided into three categories:

- geometric symbols;
- symbols of nature;
- human symbols.

In the first category we have symbols like the cross or circle, and the second includes both animal and plant symbols. Human symbols include houses, clothes and all elements that stem from human creativity.

Over millennia certain symbols have been used repeatedly as representations of certain qualities of energy and have become bedded into our collective psyche. If you carried out the exercise in Chapter 1 on linking with a quality of love you would have found a number of different symbols coming to your mind reflecting that energy. What these symbols would have told you is how you relate to that particular quality of Ch'i. To link with that energy in future you could draw upon those same symbols and that flavour of Ch'i would flow through you.

To keep this concept simple to begin with, it is better to select a few well-known symbols and try to work with them energetically. As with the colours, in time, more and more symbols can be used as you learn to extend your range of understanding. The following symbols represent a tiny selection of what is available to us. They all have been used extensively in human development, through many different cultures. They provide very good gateways to particular flavours of spiritual and healing energy.

- **Sun disk** is a powerful expansive energy that carries all the symbolism associated with the sun. It is invigorating, protective and will help you link with the spiritual side of your nature, dispelling fear and doubt.

It is said by some to be the predominant ray that Christ used within his ministry. Its all-encompassing quality makes it a very good energy to call upon when starting to learn healing. Many cultures have used the sun as a central focus to their beliefs. It was a powerful symbol within Egypt and the central symbol to the monotheistic beliefs of the Pharaoh Akhenaten.

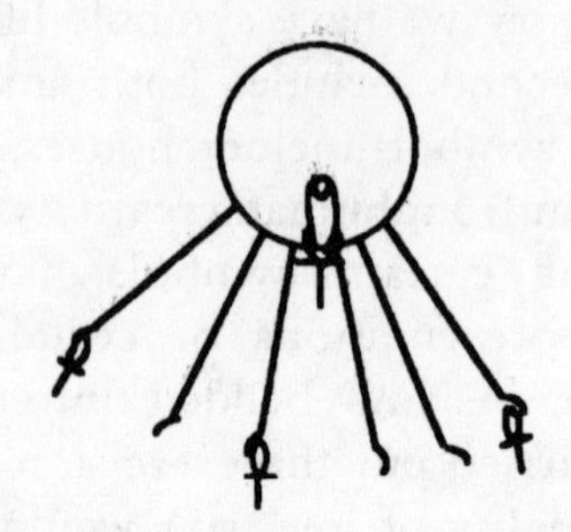

Sun Disk Symbol of Akhenaten

- **Cross** can take a number of forms. Best known are the Christian cross with its extended bottom limb and the equal armed cross. The Christian cross links with the whole development of the Christian impulse and also with the quality of self-sacrifice. Some people today find this a restrictive symbol because of some of its associations. In its equal armed form it represents the balance of the four elements, earth, air, fire and water within the physical material world. The best cross to use is in its equal armed form with the circle.
- **Cross within a circle** is an excellent symbol of balance, integration and protection. Circles have always been associated with the spirit. Combining the cross and the circle represents the link between the physical and spiritual side of our nature, so it can be used in all cases where this quality of integration is required. You can use it to balance chakric energies (see Chapter 9) and also as a general symbol to surround an individual at the end of a healing session. Its protective quality

can be very powerful if you place the symbols over areas of vulnerability or sensitivity within you or your subjects. Another form of this cross is the Celtic cross.

Celtic Cross

- **Chalice** is a symbol of renewal and replenishment. It can help link with the sensitive feminine aspect of your being and carries a very gentle quality. It is the symbol of the Holy Grail knights and as such is a most potent link with all spiritual seeking for inner wisdom. You can use it as a general healing symbol as well as providing you with a source of spiritual nourishment. Call upon it whenever you are feeling depleted in energy or low in spirits.

Chalice

- **Caduceus** (see page 77) is the symbol of the god Hermes, one of the main healing gods of the Greek pantheon. This symbol has been adopted by the medical profession today, and it represents the balance of energies as they move through the different layers within our being. Curiously, although a very ancient symbol, it also carries a close similarity to the DNA double helix molecule, which is the basic molecule of life. It can be used in all cases where balance is required, and specifically in balancing the masculine (Yang) and feminine (Yin) sides of our nature. The word hermaphrodite, which at a spiritual level represents the complete integration between the masculine and feminine principles within us, is derived from Hermes and Aphrodite, the goddess of love.

- **Rose** can be used to balance the emotional/mental sides of our nature. Roses are also sometimes associated with the four Archangels, depending on the colour. The white rose links to Michael, the yellow rose to Raphael, the red rose to Gabriel and the pink rose to Uriel. It is a very good symbol for healing all aspects connected with the heart, at a physical, emotional and spiritual level. The thorns also indicate its protective quality.
- **Lotus** is most widely known for its association with Buddhism; the Buddha generally being depicted seated on a lotus. It was also widely used in Egypt and in China. The lotus carries a powerful feeling of peace and harmony, and is another symbol that represents the link between the spiritual and physical sides of our being. It is very helpful in all cases of mental and emotional turmoil, and can provide a wonderful focus when you need to still the mind and draw inspiration from deeper layers within your being. I will often place a lotus over a person's head if they need to find peace of mind.

Lotus

- **Ankh** (see page 77) is known mainly as an ancient Egyptian symbol, but has also been found in different parts of the world. In Egypt it symbolised the life principle, but it also carries a quality of spiritual love and harmony. Because of this it can also be used for protection and transformation.
- **Six-pointed star** also carries a powerful connection with the love energy. Six was the number of perfect harmony to the Pythagorean brotherhood. It also links with the quality of inner wisdom and can provide a gateway to other dimensions within our inner world. The Star of David, with two interlocking triangles, is a representation of this symbol (see page 77).
- **Flaming sword** can be used in all cases where energy needs to be cleansed and transformed from one state to another. It is a strong, positive symbol and can be used to clear disruptive energies from around someone's energy field or alternatively to clear energies within rooms. The flaming sword is traditionally said to be wielded by the Archangel Michael.
- **Water** is also a wonderful cleansing energy that can be used physically as well as symbolically. It connects to the emotional psychic sides of our nature and can be used effectively to wash through a person's energy field to cleanse and purify it. To do this imagine a shower of gentle rain falling on someone and washing through them. It is particularly useful for those individuals who have suffered emotional trauma. It is the symbol of baptism.
- **Tree** is an excellent grounding symbol. There are many associations with trees in different cultural traditions: the Kabbalistic tree; the tree of the knowledge of good and evil in the Bible; the Scandinavian mythological tree that supported the world called the Yggdrasil; and the Bo tree under which the Buddha obtained enlightenment are only a few examples. The roots of the tree reach deep within the earth while its

branches stretch to heaven. Use this symbol whenever you sense that an individual has difficulty grounding themselves in the physical world or coming back to reality after carrying out meditative exercises.

Trees are a wonderful source of healing Ch'i. A friend of mine, after much emotional turmoil, spent a whole day sitting under a particular tree in her garden. She felt an enormous sense of relief and support coming from the tree that gave her the strength to overcome her problems. Thereafter, simply by being in its presence, she gained a feeling of inner peace.

Working with Symbols

To work with symbols you can either place the imagined symbol over your own head and draw upon its energy or you can project the symbol directly to the patient. For example, in the former case if you wished to attract a feeling of inner peace you could visualise a lotus over your head and feel that energy is flowing through you. Alternatively you could place the lotus above your subject's head to bring forward that same feeling.

I have used symbols in both ways. Generally, I work with the major archetypal symbols like the sun, Christ or specific gods or goddesses by sensing I am linking to their energy and allowing it to flow through me. Specific symbols like the caduceus I will use directly upon the patient. For example, in the latter case if I sensed an imbalance between the masculine and feminine sides of an individual's nature I might superimpose the caduceus upon them and hold that symbol in my mind for as long as it felt appropriate.

Symbols and colours can be seen as an adjunct to

healing skills. It is not necessary to use them to be a good healer, but they can extend the range of perception and quality of energy that can be directed to a patient. The exercise below gives an example of their use in healing.

EXERCISE

Using Symbols

(fifteen minutes)

***Aim**: To extend your range of perception and quality of energy through the use of symbols.*

- Sit comfortably as with all exercises and attune within. Think of one of the symbols indicated above.
- First imagine that symbol over the top of your head. Draw the energy from the symbol into yourself, and sense what you feel and experience.
- Now place the symbol under your feet and feel that you are drawing the energy up your body until you are completely surrounded by it. How does the feeling and sensation differ from the first part of the exercise?
- Next place the symbol over the area of your heart and feel you are linking your heart to the symbol, how again does this feel and what do you sense?
- Finally send out a thought of love through the symbol to a friend or member of your family and see what you experience. Gently bring yourself back to full waking reality and open your eyes.
- Write down what you experienced.

Interpreting Symbols

Interpreting symbols is a huge subject and whole books have even been devoted to just one group of symbols! It is rather like learning a new language, which, when mastered, can provide wonderfully fruitful insight into all sorts of situations. Into this category also come all the symbolic messages we receive in our dream world. An atlas of symbols can make the journey of interpretation very much easier and is strongly encouraged. A number of good reference books are given in the Bibliography at the back of this book.

Summary

- Colours and symbols act as channels or doorways to specific qualities of energy.
- They can be used by imagining that you are drawing the energy from the colour or symbol through you to the patient. Or they can be used by focusing or placing the colour or symbol directly on to the patient.
- There are many symbols and colours that can be used as aids to focusing the healing energy.
- Symbols can act as a focus for healing energy, allowing you to pick up information about the patient.

CHAPTER 7

Self-Healing And Wholeness

The wisest person
Trusts the process,
Without seeking to control;
Taking everything in their stride,
Lives not to achieve or possess,
But simply to be
All he or she can be
In harmony with Tao.

(TAO 2)

The Yin Yang Symbol

Finding wholeness within and without is one of the greatest challenges of being in a physical body. Wholeness demands balance, and balance means that we need to acknowledge and integrate all aspects of our being. There is a tendency to identify the spiritual side of ourselves with light, indeed this has been done in one of the meditation exercises in this book. However we must not forget that the greater the light the more intense the shadow and in one sense they are but two aspects of the same energy. Love and hate, joy and sadness, generosity and greed are polarity energies that reside within all of us. Wholeness means that we have to accept both sides as being part of us. If we reject one or other aspect, then imbalance occurs and illness or disharmony must result. This reconciliation of energies within the cosmos has been called the balance of yin/yang or the law of polarity. It is a good starting point for considering wholeness. As the Tao states:

> *Having and not having produce one another:*
> *Difficult and easy balance each other.*
> *Long and short complete one another.*
> *High and low rely on each other.*
> *Pitch and tone make harmony together.*
> *Beginning and ending follow each other.*
>
> (TAO 2)

The Balance of Opposites

The concept of polarity may be hard to take on board because it sometimes seems to fly in the face of conventional wisdom. Yet it has been the foundation stone of many cultures and belief systems. The Buddha exhorted his followers to take the Noble Middle Path. The only way that we can achieve this is by acknowledging the polarities that exist on either side. Some schools of thought suggest that wholeness is a state beyond polarity or duality. I would prefer to see wholeness as a perfect balance between polarities, a state of being where we are free to choose how we express ourselves, rather than being sucked into one side or the other. A quick exercise demonstrates this point.

EXERCISE

Balancing

(two minutes)

***Aim**: To demonstrate balance.*

- Stand up and place your two feet slightly apart. Close your eyes and feel the balance between each foot.
- Bring your feet together and then slowly raise one foot off the ground, keeping it there for as long as you can. Observe what happens.
- Sit down when you have finished.

Sooner or later the raised foot has to come down to create balance. It will often come down quite forcibly, as we topple, which also happens in real life. If we put ourselves into one polarity, without acknowledging the other, we will eventually be pulled, sometimes violently, into its opposite. Think about your own life. When has this happened to you? Finding wholeness means that we have to be open to working with both polarities, either through yourself or through another.

Evolution moves forward. If we stand still we are in effect going backwards. To walk forward means that we have to move from one foot to the next, one polarity to the next. As long as a balance is maintained no problem occurs. If you get out of balance you will stumble, rather like a runner who catches a foot against a stone. Walking meditations can be a marvellous exercise for finding this balance within.

Extremes

The symbol of balance in Ancient China is the yin/yang. In Chinese thought everything was seen as a weaving together of these two energies. Within extreme yang there is yin and vice versa. If you move into an extreme position you will eventually flip into its opposite or be challenged by its opposite through another. If you seek love and peace, yet deny the hate and turmoil within, then you will be either drawn into experiencing those emotions, or be confronted by others that express them back to you.

Dr Roger Woolger, in his book *'Other Lives, Other Selves'*, has noted how often individuals will move from being persecutor in one life to victim in the next and then back to persecutor again, as though caught in a spiral that pulls them first one way and then the next. Resolution can only come when we acknowledge that we are both victim and persecutor. The more that we reach into the light, the more that we need to own our shadow.

Not all polarities reach these extremes. You can be artistic or not artistic, musical or not musical, mathematical or not mathematical and either state is OK. As in the walking analogy above, we have to move from one polarity to the other in order to experience. This is a natural part of life. After all, we are born either as men or women and although a state of androgyny might be seen as desirable by some, it would also deny us valuable opportunities for growth. In an ideal partnership or marriage a balance of energies is maintained, with each party carrying an aspect of the polarity. There are many skills that we possess that can be used to complement the talents of our partners and those around us. The key to life is knowing whether you feel comfortable or not comfortable with yourself; at ease or in a state of dis-ease, with any part of who and what you are. If we are at ease with ourselves then we will 'follow our bliss' as Joseph Cambell so aptly put it. To achieve this we must address those aspects that cause dis-ease, at whatever level they manifest.

Polarities move through all walks of life. The present party political structure in Britain reflects these twin forces. One party represents the individual, the other the collective and the third seeks the middle ground between them. Both sides are important. By working with these polarities a form of consensus should emerge. If either of the main parties moves too far in one direction or the other then a new election reverses the process. The difficulties are that ideologies are sometimes difficult to change. The Capitalist system has something valuable to offer as does the Socialist. The collapse of Communism came not from external pressures from the West, but from within, because it had reached an extreme position. Capitalism also faces grave challenges, particularly in the form of unemployment, which will eventually force it to reverse some of its present trends. As Carl Jung observed the cosmos demands wholeness. Interestingly it is claimed in the '*Theories of Complexity*' that the greatest changes, innovations and transformations occur at the threshold between order and chaos. The apparent chaos in so many present world situations may actually be more hopeful than it seems.

As part of the self-healing process we need to begin to understand how these polarities are working individually within us. The following exercise can help us with this.

EXERCISE

Polarity

(ten minutes)

***Aim**: To determine how polarities are working through your life.*

- Take a sheet of plain white paper and divide it into four equal squares as illustrated.
- Into the top left-hand square write down all those aspects of yourself that you see as your desirable and good qualities. These could be such things as 'I am a good cook', 'I am a good father/mother', 'I am generous' etc.
- Into the bottom left-hand square write down all those aspects that you see as your undesirable or bad qualities. These could be such things as 'I am always late', 'I am untidy', ' I am selfish' etc.
- Next compare the length of the two lists. Is the list in the top square the same length as the list in the bottom square? If not something is amiss in your life. With many people the list in the bottom left square can often be more than double that of the one above it. This is not balanced.
- Now the fun begins. In the top right-hand square write down the opposites of what you wrote in the top left. Taking the examples above this could be 'I am a bad cook', 'I am a bad father/mother', 'I am selfish'.
- Into the bottom right-hand square again write the opposites, which in this case might be 'I am punctual', 'I am tidy', 'I am generous'.
- Now take a coloured pencil and draw a box

around the two right-hand squares. This is your shadow side.

- For the final part of this exercise, think closely about your life and see if you are aware how each of the polarities that you have written down operates within you. If you feel you are a good cook, when has something happened, may be an important dinner party, where everything went wrong. What was the dynamic that caused this to happen?

As you can see from the above exercise your shadow contains both desirable and undesirable qualities. What you must realise is that if you do not own or acknowledge them then someone else close to you will carry them for you. They have to, as part of cosmic balance. Your shadow contains an enormously rich source of material. Those elements that you see as your failings, in the bottom left-hand square, if reversed, can become a

Polarity Chart

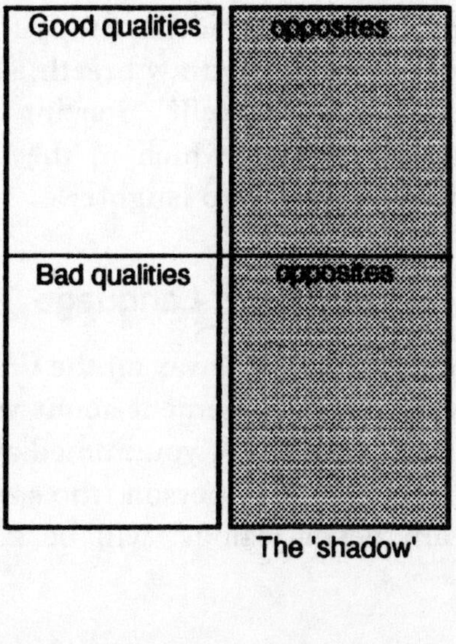

Good qualities	opposites
Bad qualities	opposites

The 'shadow'

fountain of great strength. As they are a part of you, you can take them back and incorporate them consciously into your life. It might require a bit of effort, but that will make them all the more worth while. Within this, we also need to acknowledge those polarity sides that we have chosen to work with in this particular life. As a man I cannot suddenly give birth to children, but I can acknowledge the feminine within me.

You also need to be very mindful of the polarities to the top left-hand square. As long as you acknowledge those opposites or the potential for those opposites to occur there will be no problem. As soon as you deny that possibility then you invite that opposite into your life. It is bound to happen sooner or later.

I once heard a good example of this on the radio from a famous musician. He had been performing a very difficult work at a major concert in America and had been playing beautifully. Three-quarters of the way through the concert, he suddenly thought to himself 'Aren't I doing well?' The very next stanza he missed his notes, and felt so mortified that he could not face anyone after the concert and it took him a long time even to mention it again. Life has a way of making us face the opposites within. A friend of mine very narrowly, and through great skill, missed having a car accident. Stopping the car, and sitting to collect herself and draw breath, she said to her friends 'Didn't I do that well?' Starting up again she drove straight into a tree, which in the circumstances made all of them collapse into laughter.

Polarities in Language

Your language will give you away all the time. As soon as you make any definitive statement about yourself, 'I am always . . .', 'I am never . . .', you immediately invite the opposite into your life. The person who says 'I am never angry' or 'I am never jealous' will be surrounded by angry or jealous people. Try and observe this with your friends, although they may not always thank you if you point this out to them. See how it operates within your own life. When you acknowledge or balance any energy within you, those people who are expressing the opposite have to change in their relationship to you because the resonances within you have altered. In some cases this may mean them going out of your life.

Mental attitudes, and the way we express them through our language, are a powerful determinate in our life. Unfortunately we often carry mental affirmations from childhood. Siblings in a family sometimes get labelled as being 'no good at sport, art, singing'. They will then carry these labels into adult life as 'truths' abou themselves. When this happens you can sometimes unconsciously invite someone into your life who reinforces this belief by continually presenting the opposite. These dynamics happen on many occasions in relationships, where individuals move into extreme positions. For example, the partner who is clever at DIY can end up with someone who cannot mend a fuse. As long as each feels comfortable in this position then everything is fine. However, it can easily degenerate into one partner feeling totally incompetent and the other arrogantly capable. As soon as this happens problems are bound to ensue. You can easily check any situation, emotion or attitude that is part of your life by asking the simple question 'Am I at ease with this situation or not?' If not the dis-ease surrounding it must be addressed and not swept under the carpet.

Keys to Balance

Paradoxically it could be argued that ease and dis-ease are but two sides of a polarity, and both need to be expressed in your life. This is surely why the Buddha preached nonattachment. Yet you are in a physical body, and need to appreciate and balance the wonderful experiences that it gives you. If dis-ease is present try and understand why it is there, and what needs to be done to move to a state of wholeness.

The key to solving such situations is continually to acknowledge the opposites within you. This is why affirmations can be so powerful and effective. In the example given above, instead of feeling totally incompetent, the individual needs to affirm that he or she is competent and to acknowledge those areas where this is so. You are always a mixture and can find balance by seeing those opposites working through you. As soon as you affirm your ability to be both competent and incompetent it ceases to be a problem. The partner will then be forced into a similar stance, for as soon as one partner shifts the other has to shift also. How this is accommodated in any relationship will be dependent upon the individuals in question. In some cases it may be necessary to separate, in others a new form of relationship can be found. Being aware of potential relationship problems should be an important ingredient in any therapy session.

EXERCISE

Affirmations

(ten minutes)

Aim: *To balance opposites within.*

- Begin to think about what quality you need to balance within your life. Let us say that you have a problem with shyness.

- Reflect on what shyness means to you. What are its causes? Often fear can be at the bottom of many such problems. Reflect on what you perceive is the opposite of shyness and think of someone in your life who appears to express the opposite.
- List down on a piece of paper where shyness operates within your life. Think also of where it is an advantage and where is it a disadvantage to you.
- On the same piece of paper write down where the opposite of shyness operates within your life. Perhaps with your closest friends. What word or sentence best describes this quality of feeling. You might decide that something like 'I am confident and open with whoever I meet', best describes this feeling.
- Next carry out the **body awareness exercise** and connect with your inner light.
- Acknowledge the part of you that is shy and thank that part for all that it has taught you. Try to accept it as part of yourself.
- Now repeat your affirmation aloud, 'I am confident and open with whoever I meet' and imagine yourself acting from this new position in different situations. Try to hold the picture together with the words in your mind.
- When you have affirmed this statement a number of times, bring yourself back to full waking consciousness.
- Whenever you are in situations that test your shyness, first acknowledge the part of you that is shy then repeat in your imagination the affirmation and see yourself being confident.

Polarities are also very important within your feeling or emotional life. Culturally in the West we are encouraged to believe that certain emotions are good and others are bad. This has brought forth a tendency to consider feelings like jealousy, anger and resentment as being evil and unacceptable. They become something to be avoided or suppressed at all costs. Unfortunately you cannot deal with emotions in this way. You can only find balance by fully acknowledging that energy within you. Suppress it and it will come out as a dis-ease at one level or another. This does not mean to say that you need to act out all your emotions. You might feel so angry with someone that you just wish to punch them on the nose. Acting this out is an inappropriate way of dealing with this anger. It is much better to punch a cushion, and even more so to sit quietly and really feel into this energy, accepting it as part of yourself, before allowing it to dissipate away from you. When you have really accepted an energy it will cease to have any hold over you and will therefore no longer be a problem. **Acceptance is not resignation but a very positive act of consciousness**.

As the Tao tells us:

The Tao person knows himself
And makes no show,
Accepts himself
And is not arrogant.

(TAO 72)

All emotions can have their beneficial sides. It was not feeling happy and contented that drove Bob Geldof into forming Band Aid, but because he was very angry about what was going on. His anger was channelled into constructive use. There are situations where fear is a very appropriate energy and helps preserve us from life-threatening situations. The more that you can feel OK with your emotions, and how and why you express them, the less will they be a problem in your life. They become a source of powerful nourishment. Our aim should be to be happy with being unhappy, joyful at being sad, contented when we feel discontented and trusting when we feel fear. Whatever the emotion it then becomes a valuable experience that allows you to affirm most powerfully, 'This is me'. In this way energies pass through us, enriching our lives and all that we do. If we can willingly enter into the pit of despond then we can reach the most sublime heights of consciousness and being, but we cannot have one without the other. I have known individuals experience moments of great ecstasy and bliss, only to be subsequently thrown into deep depression wondering what was wrong. All that the cosmos asks is that we be prepared to experience both. As long as we can acknowledge both parts of us then we are free to move into either polarity. Indeed, some of the greatest creativity has come out of depression. As the Tao states:

> *The way to greatest light leads*
> *through shadow.*
>
> (TAO 41)

Exhaustion

Dis-ease also occurs when we deliberately resist or suppress energies that need to be part of us. Consider the humble electric fire. It provides us with warmth because an electric current passes through a length of wire. The wire gets hot because of its resistance to the current. Step up the flow of energy and it burns out. In a similar way when we resist an energy it creates a heat within. Over-resist and we become inflamed with pain and suffering. We all need a certain amount of resistance for in this way we learn about different qualities of energy. Difficulties occur when we over-resist or, as happens in many cases, try to block the energy completely. **The main cause of pain is resistance. If you are suffering in any way, ask yourself 'What am I resisting?' 'What am I blocking?'** This resistance is also a major contributory factor in a prevalent problem that faces many people today, that of exhaustion.

Chronic Fatigue Syndrome (ME) and similar conditions are caused by a breakdown in flows of Ch'i between different aspects within the psyche. With ME there is certainly a physical cause, a virus of some description, but this can be seen to be the result of imbalances in Ch'i on other levels. In many cases this is caused by a resistance to some aspect within the life. Usually it is because the 'ego' mind is at odds with the spiritual self. Recovery generally follows fairly quickly when shifts at this level have been made. Always be open to look at what you might be resisting and what you need to change. The greater the resistance the greater the effort. No wonder we get tired. In our fire analogy an increase in current can easily be accommodated by changing the wire to another material or by making it thicker. As the Tao reminds us:

Follow the ancient wisdom:
'Yield and Overcome.'
True peace is achieved
By centring
And merging with Life.
(TAO 22)

The lethargy of resistance has a very different feel from energy being drained out of us by another person. In the latter case the feeling of tiredness usually happens very suddenly. As we have seen, some professionals, like teachers and healthcare workers, are prone to this type of energy depletion. Their tiredness at the end of the day has been caused by a continual draining of Ch'i.

Protection and, more important, energy re-charge will adequately deal with this problem. Resisting energies that need to flow through you takes a lot of effort which is why we get tired.

We also need to recognise that the physical body has its needs. Correct inputs in the form of the food we eat, exercise and so on play their part. Most doctors would ascribe a sudden drop in energy to a chemical imbalance within the body. At a physical level this is correct. But just as a feeling of fear causes an immediate adrenalin input into the body, so also a depletion in the subtle energies will produce a chemical change. There is always an interconnecting correspondence between the many layers within.

To balance our emotions and free up our resistances we can use an adaptation of the **polarity balancing exercise** given in Chapter 3.

EXERCISE

Balancing Resistances

(five to ten minutes)

Aim: *To integrate those aspects of yourself that you are resisting.*

- Carry out the first part of the **polarity balancing exercise** given in Chapter 3, but this time imagine that the energy you are resisting is on one side of your body or the other. Try and visualise it as a colour or feeling. Go and sit in it, feel it, experience it, breathe it in and acknowledge it as being part of you. Then move into the opposite polarity and do the same.

- Finally balance the energy by finding the mid-point between the two.
- Write down or draw a picture of your experiences.

The important thing when you experience any emotion is not to reject it and consider that it is somehow undesirable. If you wake up in the morning feeling sad, angry, resentful or whatever, give yourself the space to be with that energy. If it is not appropriate at that minute, you can set aside a period at some time during the day to acknowledge it. Doing this will free up energies within and provide a balance in your life.

Look at Your Emotional Responses

It is very easy to test what is relevant to your life and what is not by looking at your emotional responses either to situations, individuals or the things people say. Energy will always flow where there is a resonant connection. If someone makes a statement to you, there are three ways that you will assess it:

- you will agree with it;
- you will be indifferent to it;
- you will reject it.

If you are indifferent to it then it does not connect to you at a resonant level. If you feel enthusiastic for it or strongly opposed to it, then it has a resonant connection. Both of these two, from a point of wholeness, are important. Our tendency is to turn our back on those things that we are opposed to or dislike. Balance asks that we look closely at those things we reject, for there is always an element of truth there that needs to be acknowledged. Our resistance occurs because we find it hard to accept that truth. The next time someone makes a comment to you and you feel a strong emotional response, ask yourself 'Why am I feeling this?' 'What is the underlying condition that I may not be recognising?'

A friend of mine was confronted by a particular problem in her life. To understand what was happening she carried out a meditation where she imagined she was in a theatre. She asked within that the cause of her difficulty be presented to her on the stage. At this point the stage floor opened up and a hideous, slimy figure emerged, saying that he was Sloth and Envy. Somewhat shocked, my friend in her mind said 'Why are you here? You have nothing to do with me'. 'Oh yes I have', said the figure, and then proceeded to tell her all the areas in her life where he had been present. Owning this energy, this side of herself, was a traumatic experience, but a very necessary one for my friend to integrate this aspect within.

Conversely, when someone makes a comment to you like 'you are always a mess', do not fall into the trap of accepting this totally. Only part of it will be true. A comment of this nature was made to a colleague of mine on a number of occasions by a particular individual. Feeling somewhat miffed his initial response was that the observation was total rubbish. He knew many examples that demonstrated the opposite. However, upon reflection he had to concede that there was an element of truth in what was being said. There were some areas that gave grounds for the statement. By being conscious and aware of this, he could then take steps to correct this fault. In doing this he became very aware that the individual in question had a similar fault which he was just projecting on to others. **It is very important to realise that the faults we see in others are but the faults that exist in ourselves.** We should be open to accepting that which is ours, but no more than that.

Your Outer World Mirrors Your Inner Reality

The next idea follows on from this. Your outer world that includes your friends, colleagues, enemies and all the things that happen to you is a reflection of whom and what you are inside. If you wish to judge how well you are doing in your life, look at all the elements – the people and situations that are around you. Are they balanced? Are they healthy? Those that are not will immediately tell you where your imbalances lie within and we all have imbalances at some level or another.

Outer world reflects your inner world

One way of looking at this is to imagine that we have within us a number of characters. Sometimes these are referred to as sub-personalities. The Ch'i from our soul or spiritual self comes down through the centre of our being and is reflected out through these sub-personalities. Imagine that they are each playing a different piece of music. Because of the law of resonance (like attracts like), we will draw to us those people who most closely match the music that the characters within are playing. So, metaphorically, if one of your characters is playing 'rhythm and blues' you will attract an individual into your outer world that is also playing 'rhythm and blues'. Resonances will be set up and energy will flow between you. There is a wonderful quote from Thackeray's *Vanity Fair* expressing this idea that goes:

> *The world is a looking-glass, and gives back to every man the reflection of his own face. Frown at it, and it will in turn look sourly upon you; laugh at it and with it, and it is a jolly kind companion; and so let all young persons take their choice.*

You can therefore look upon your outer world as a mirror to your inner life. The images that you see are aspects of yourself overlaid on to other people. This is a challenging thought for it means that all significant events in your life have in some way an intrinsic connection with the dynamic of your inner self. In other words you have, at some level within your psyche, drawn all your experiences to you and therefore must accept responsibility for them.

This idea does need to be qualified. If a person, through their free will, suddenly chooses to take a gun and shoots at a large number of people at random, killing some of them, the people in question would not necessarily have deliberately chosen to go through such an experience. Part of the hazard of living in a physical body, in our present society, is to take the risk of having our free will abused. It would equally be totally wrong to lay the blame for a child abuser on the child.

However, it is interesting to see how often, when major accidents or catastrophes occur, that many people manage to avoid being killed. It is as though the spiritual self, in these cases, is aware of the impending problem and creates a protection for the life.

A strong example of intervention from the spiritual self occurred among the choir of the church in the little farming town of Beatrice in Nebraska in 1950. The choir, numbering 15 people, used to meet regularly every Tuesday evening at 7.20 p.m. On one particular Tuesday, in March, all 15 members of the choir were at least ten minutes late, which was just as well, for at 7.25 p.m that night, the boiler exploded in the church demolishing everything. The likelihood of this happening, with all of them being late on the same night, has been calculated as one chance in a million. This assumed that some members were normally late from time to time. This could be put down to just an extraordinary coincidence, which would be perfectly reasonable, if it were not a pattern that has been repeated elsewhere on many occasions. A more plausible suggestion is that at some level of consciousness the members of the choir were aware of what was going to happen and therefore avoided being present.

In the second case a friend of mine was involved with a group of people converting a barn. For no apparent reason, at a specific moment all of them fled the building in a panic. The next instant a large beam of timber from the roof came crashing down on the spot where many of them had been standing. Was this coincidence again or a sixth sense that warned them in time? It is my belief that the more we are in touch with these deeper layers of our being, the more likely we are to be protected from such situations.

While some 'accidents' do occur, I am sure that the vast array of experiences that happen within your life have arisen because you attracted them to you. This means that it is no good blaming others for our misfortunes.

The following exercise will give some insights into this dynamic and the part played by others in our life.

EXERCISE

Mirroring

(ten minutes)

Aim: *To obtain insights about ourselves by studying our friends.*

- Write down a list of some of the people you get on well with and who are important in your life.
- Think about these people. What is it that attracts you to them?
- Next write down three things that pleases you in their personality and three things that you find difficult about them.
- In what way do you see the qualities you have written down existing within you, both as similarities and their opposites? For example if one of the things you like about a friend is their generosity, in what way are you generous and what way are you stingy? If one of the things that you dislike about a friend is that they are always late, consider in what ways you are both late and punctual.

- Now repeat the exercise with some individuals whom you find difficult to get on with.
- When you have finished compare the two lists. Are there any underlying common themes?

Remember, if you either like or dislike an individual there has to be a resonant connection between you. The stronger the feeling is the stronger the connection will be. The people you hate express the things that you hate about yourself. The people you love express the things that you love about yourself. This resonating connection can stem either from environmental patterning, genetic patterning or from past life experiences. When some difficult situation comes into your life, you need to ask yourself why you have attracted this to you? What is it that I have to learn from this experience? This can be difficult to do because it is often much easier to wallow in self-pity. But sooner or later we have to face up to the situation. I know within my own life when I have avoided looking at these questions it has caused difficulties. How much easier it would have been if I had dealt with it at the earliest opportunity.

Balancing Relationships

How do we balance up these problems? The simplest way is to work with them in our inner world. Tradition tells us that there are two ways to transform these types of situations. The first is by loving them, as Christ said **'Turn the other cheek'** or, as abounds in fairy tales, like the *Frog Prince*, or *Beauty and the Beast*. The second is by standing up to them and this is encapsulated in the many hero myths like Perseus and Medusa, and St George and the dragon. The case studies below demonstrate these two approaches. What is very important, before carrying out any inner balancing work of this type, is to first make contact with your own inner spiritual source for guidance on what needs to be done. Perseus gained the help of the gods when he went to slay Medusa, and from the blood of her body sprang the white winged horse Pegasus. Interestingly, the constellation of Pegasus, a symbol of transformation, sits exactly on the cusp of Pisces and Aquarius. As we move from one age to the next humanity will have to transform its own Medusa state (mindlessness), to negotiate the transition.

Two examples of balancing the dynamic of relationships come to mind from my own life. The first occurred at school when I was about 15 with a particular individual who started to pick on me in a bullying way. This went on for a period, getting more and more unpleasant, until I decided to do something about it. Now conventional wisdom suggests that we need to be able to stand up to such people, but at the time I adopted a different approach. I sat at a desk and wrote down all the good qualities that I could see in this person and then visualised strongly those qualities coming from him. Within a couple of days his whole attitude changed and we became firm friends.

The next example occurred many years later when I was working under contract with a particular builder. He had a very violent temper which he used to great effect to intimidate people. He also had many likeable qualities but his anger terrified me, as it did others. This feeling of fear reached a level where it was starting to interfere with my job, making me dislike going into work. Eventually I realised that this had to stop, I could avoid it no longer. So one evening I invited him into my inner world by visualising him in front of me. Seeing his good sides did not seem to be appropriate here, but meeting his anger did. I realised that I had to call upon all my inner strength to not be brow-beaten by this energy, which is what I did. Although he had never lost his temper directly at me before, a couple of days later he came storming into my office, in a violent rage and laid into me about something that was in no way my fault or responsibility. The effect was to make me get angry back and stand up to him. The response was amazing. His jaw dropped and he stepped back, mumbled a few words and then left the office, sending an apology later through another individual. From that moment I had no more problems working with him. In both these cases by working within I had transformed my outer world.

The principle behind this is quite simple. Change your inner world and your outer world has to follow suit. If this involves an individual the dynamic between you has to shift.

The following exercise will help you balance up those difficult qualities that friends, colleagues, parents, siblings, neighbours or acquaintances display towards you. In carrying out this exercise it is very important to realise that the individuals you are working on are actually an aspect of yourself. They are all a reflection of your sub-personalities. You are only using them as a focus to balance up your inner world. The aim is not to heal the person out there, but to heal the person within you. You will need to select one individual for this exercise, but it can be repeated again at another time with as many others as you choose.

EXERCISE

Relationship Balancing

(ten minutes)

***Aim**: To balance relationships with your friends, colleagues or members of your family.*

- Adopt your normal meditation posture, close your eyes and carry out the technique for connecting with your inner light.
- Bring to mind the individual whom you wish to work upon and see them sitting there in front of you.
- Next, think of the problem that surrounds this individual. In what way is it part of yourself? Why do you feel it is difficult?
- Ask from within for help in dealing with this situation.
- Now determine whether you have to reverse your perception of this individual or overcome your fear and stand up to them.
- In the former case surround them with love and in your mind reverse all the qualities that appear to be coming from them. For example, if they are treating you in a mean way, see them as generous and open hearted, and so on.
- In the latter case call upon all your strength and feel that you have sufficient energy to meet theirs. See yourself as clear and strong in your own space.
- When you have completed this part, imagine that you are lifting the person in question up into an imaginary light above you.
- Thank the spiritual forces for their help and slowly bring yourself back to full waking consciousness.

These types of exercises are very powerful. The more time and energy that you put into them the more dramatic they will be. You might need to work on some situations more than once. Each attempt will help you deepen the experience. It can also be very helpful to have a friend, colleague or therapist take you through them, particularly if you are confronting a major situation or problem within your life. To have the support of others around us is very beneficial. However it is also important to realise that no matter how powerful or difficult a situation may seem you will always have sufficient strength to deal with it at this inner level. This is a cosmic principle.

Parent and Child

There is one other type of energetic exercise that can be very helpful in dealing with past situations. It relates particularly to our parents, or those people who have been closely associated with us, perhaps over many incarnations. In these cases an energy vortex gets built, carrying all the memories of what has happened between you. This can take on a life of its own. In consequence, as soon as we connect with that person, this pattern of energy overrides everything. It therefore has the effect of clouding or preventing any new association or a change in the relationship. Parents become a prime candidate for this because very often they will, either consciously or unconsciously, see their offspring as small children. Individuals are then forced into the parent/child role so clearly described in transactional analysis. The adult in us might wish to exert itself and probably does in most other areas of our life. But as soon as we are back at home this old pattern emerges. Paradoxically, sometimes you will see a switch taking place where the child takes on the role of parent, and forces the parent into being the child. Many famous comedy situations like *Steptoe and Son* are based on this type of scenario, where both vie with each other to be the parent.

These Ch'i webs need to be cut and transformed. There are a number of different techniques that can be adopted to achieve this de-linking process, one of which is included here. I have used it for many different types of situation, including karmic problems. It can be adapted wherever you feel there is an undesirable link between yourself and another person. What effectively you are doing is healing the energy pattern that has been created between you.

EXERCISE

De-Linking Emotional and Mental Bonds

(ten minutes)

Aim: *To free up the ties of past patterning in relationships.*

- Adopt your normal meditation posture and connect with your inner light.
- Next think of the individual with whom you wish to cut the undesirable links and imagine that they are sitting in a chair opposite you.
- Connect to them at their highest level. To do this you can imagine that there is a light above and between both of you. Visualise a golden thread linking to this light and down again to the individual. In that way you will still maintain your spiritual link with the person, which will allow a new form of relationship to take place.
- Imagine that there is a cord of energy linking from your solar plexus to that of the other individual. Sometimes this is visualised as a rope, but with others this energy can be

visualised as chains, thick logs, umbilical cords and iron bars, to name but a few.

- You will need to sever or cut this energy. To do so use whatever symbol is most appropriate in relation to how you imagined this energy to be. For example, if you visualised it as a rope, a sword or sharp knife would do. Keep cutting in your mind for as long as you feel the energy is held. It might take several strokes of the sword or knife before the rope is severed.
- When cut, imagine that you are absorbing the loose end back into yourself and then send a thought of healing to help the other person absorb their end within themselves in a balanced way.
- Next imagine that you are within your own sphere of light and they are within theirs as two separate individuals who can now relate to each other in a new way.
- Finally carry out the forgiveness exercise mentioned in Chapter 2 and thank that individual for all that they have taught you.

With deep-seated cases you may need to carry out this exercise on a number of occasions before the links are finally severed. It will not mean that you are disconnecting from the person completely, only that you will be changing the pattern of how you relate to them.

Phobias and Fears

All phobias and fears can be treated at an imagery level, providing there is a willingness to do so. Neuro-linguistic programming (NLP) and hypnotism have achieved much in these areas, as have regression work and past life therapies. Providing the spiritual self participates great changes and healing can occur. If the soul does not wish to change, for whatever reason, the person will soon revert back to where they were before. Sometimes we need to be patient in allowing these shifts to come about. Such changes can be assisted by a therapist or we can work upon them ourselves.

Many years ago one of my students overcame her dread of water by participating in a meditation class that spent some of the time in visualisation exercises connected with water. When, in her mind, she could stand quite happily under a waterfall, all fear of the water went, to the extent that she then learned to swim.

The solution is always to confront the fear at an inner level. If you can do this successfully it will no longer be a problem in your outer world. The same applies to traumatic situations that have occurred. As hard as it is at times healing will only come about fully when we can go back inside ourselves and confront the trauma at an imagery level.

The above systems of balancing exercise are more geared to the emotional, mental and psychological aspects of our being. If you have a chronic illness almost certainly one or other of these levels will be involved. However, it is also important not to neglect the physical side of ourselves. Apart from normal balancing exercises that should become part of your daily routine, you can also give specific healing to parts that are causing you difficulty. You need to be mindful from studies in the US that the most effective healing occurs when the healer works upon the whole person rather than the specific. This is why balancing all your energies is important. However, if you do have a sprained ankle you can in addition send healing directly to the ankle.

EXERCISE

Physical Self Healing

(five minutes)

Aim: *To self-heal physical conditions.*

There are two approaches you can adopt. The easiest method is to hold your hand or hands over or near the troublesome spot. Then send energy as though you were giving healing to another person. Maintain this flow for as long as you feel is necessary. You will find that you can considerably speed up the healing of burns, scalds and wounds of all descriptions.

The second method is a little more complex. In this you need to imagine that you are stepping out of your body and then giving healing to yourself as though you were giving healing to a patient. This method can be effective for those areas like the middle of the back that are not easily reachable with your hands.

Alternatively, simply directing energy through your mind to the affected part is also a good method to use. As healers we should not be averse to receiving treatment from others. It is a trap to think that we have to do it all ourselves. But if you have the tools available, why not use them?

To change and grow in life we have to meet many challenges. This means that we need to spend time balancing and harmonising the various elements within. This should become a daily routine. It need not take up a long period of time each day. Five to ten minutes is all that is necessary, but it will be time well spent. There will always be moments when we need help from others. We should not forget that life is made up of both giving and receiving. Seeking help from others when we are in crisis is very important and as healers we should not be too proud to do this.

Summary

- For the final part of this exercise, think closely about your life and see if you are aware how each of the polarities that you have written down operates within you. If you feel you are a good cook, when has something happened, may be an important dinner party, where everything went wrong. What was the dynamic that caused this to happen? Wholeness demands that you need to accept all elements within.
- Life is made up of polarities that flow through all aspects of yourself. You need to acknowledge both the light and shadow sides of your nature.
- The key to solving difficult situations is continually to acknowledge the opposites within them.
- Events and people in your outer world mirror your inner life.
- Change the inner world and the outer has to follow suit.
- One of the main causes of dis-ease is resistance to energies that need to flow through us.

CHAPTER 8

Developing Your Psychic Senses

Take heed of details
And develop great insight.

(TAO 52)

Diagnostic Techniques

Two Directions of Ch'i

Ch'i in relationship to yourself can travel in two directions. It is both received (yin) and projected from you (yang). In Ancient China every aspect of life was seen as a reflection of either yang or yin energy. In this sense, men are yang and women yin, the day is yang the night is yin, the sky is yang and the earth is yin and so on. We still have a reflection of this type of concept in the French language which gives a gender for common nouns such as *la porte* (the door) feminine or *le toit* (the roof) masculine.

When working with Ch'i you need to be mindful of these two flows. It is important to learn to harness and develop both aspects in balance within you. In the Tao it was recognised that even within extreme yang there was yin and vice versa. The ideal is to try to find a level of balance between all aspects of ourselves, yet recognising that perfect balance within us is an impossibility in the physical world. We therefore have to value our imperfections and see them as stepping stones to a greater understanding of life.

When you send out healing Ch'i from yourself to help another you are working strongly on the yang polarity. But to be energetically balanced you need also to develop the receptive side of yourself. This will help you become more aware of how you can best assist when sending healing and also what to say or not to say when helping friends. Trusting the process when you first commence your healing training is very important. Yet evolution demands that eventually you must start to take responsibility for what comes through you, just as doctors have to take responsibility for the medicines they prescribe. In expressing healing Ch'i in a yang way you need to develop the yin aspect of your consciousness so that you can quickly determine the inner causes of any condition. You will then know what is the right flavour and quality of energy that you need to draw upon.

The yin aspect of your being will also help you connect to your inner wisdom; the Tao within. This helps enormously in all aspects of decision making where you need to determine the most beneficial route to take. I recently heard of a very successful business person who never made any important business decisions without first consulting the I Ching. Very often, what separates the very successful entrepreneur from his of her peers is an instinct or inner knowing of whether to act or not. During this chapter we will look at ways to develop this ability.

Developing Both Sides of Your Polarity

Just as you are born either as a man (yang) or a woman (yin), so also at a psychic level you will either be predominantly yang or yin. That is to say you will either be better at sending out Ch'i or receiving it. This has nothing to do with gender, but arises from the balance of energy that the soul or spiritual self has chosen to express in this particular life. So, at a psychic level some men and women will naturally favour a yang expression in their healing work while others will be yin. This means that some healers are better transmitters of energy while some are better receivers of energy or information. This preference was noted in Professor Rhine's telepathy studies described in Chapter 1. If you work within a healing group look around at the healers and see how they are working. What quality of strength does each carry? Those who are better senders will often find it difficult to pick up information, but will often get the best results. Those who pick up well will gain plenty of information about a patient, perhaps some of the causes of their suffering. But they will not necessarily be effective in helping them shift their conditions. It is not necessary to begin with to know which side of the spectrum your natural energy lies, for this will soon come out as you start to develop your healing skills. However, in broad terms if you are a naturally sensitive person affected by moods and energies of others you will almost certainly reflect the yin polarity. Conversely, if you move through life seemingly oblivious to these subtle forces but have a knack of 'making things happen', then you will most likely be on the yang polarity.

You need to strive to find an integration between these two aspects of your being. The challenge for the yang healer is how to develop the yin side of themselves or how to pick up more information about their patient. The challenge for the yin healer is the opposite. Many yin healers find their way into counselling or psychotherapy, for this is a natural expression of their receptive sense. However, one of the problems that some counsellors face in these circumstances is a neglect of their yang polarity. In consequence they become over-sensitive and can easily be drained or affected by their clients. The solution is to learn to develop their yang qualities, especially working on protection and channelling the positive psychic energy.

Developing the receptive side of yourself is not such a difficult task if approached in the right way, although some yang psychics can find this problematic. In my case, my natural energy is yang, so I have had to work quite hard to express the other side of my polarity. The solution has been to develop an extensive number of different techniques that I can call upon, so that if I get stuck at one level I have other options.

Our psychic abilities will naturally wax and wane in a cyclical pattern. Most long-standing healers and psychics are only too aware of those days when everything seems spot on, while on others it is very hard to hit the mark. There will be times when energy will flow very easily and times when it will not. In an ideal world we would schedule our work in accordance with these rhythms, but in practice we often have to work when our skills are not at their optimum. This is where specific techniques, such as those set out below, become valuable.

The Four Levels of Being

One simple classification that I have already suggested, in looking at ourselves, is to recognise the four layers of our being. These are the physical, emotional, mental and spiritual sides of yourself. These four aspects correlate with the four elements of earth, water, air and fire, and the four qualities that Jung described of sensation, feeling, thinking and intuition. This classification becomes helpful when we appreciate how we can readily use any or all of these energy bodies to pick up information. As has already been emphasised, any energy inputs will cause a resonance within, that will immedi-

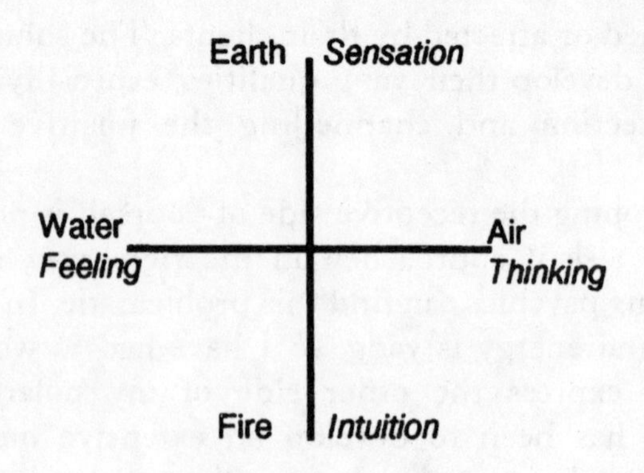

Table of correspondences

ately be translated across all spectrums. Therefore, to pick up insights on the causes of conditions, we can learn to tap into each or any of these four levels. Each has its own well-recognised set of techniques, for example, dowsing or divining is an aspect of the physical or sensation side of our being.

In practice individuals tend to gravitate to one level and then stick with it. They might find that they have a reasonable ability to receive clairvoyant pictures but have not bothered to develop any other technique. The problem with this is that, if they are having an off day on their clairvoyance, they have nothing to fall back upon. These four elements of sensation, feeling, thinking and intuition will now be discussed in greater detail in relation to our diagnostic abilities.

Physical Receptivity

The densest layer of your being is your physical body. This acts like a resonating sounding board to information that you receive, which in turn can be translated into two forms. First, you can develop an awareness of different sensations and their location within the body. For example, when giving healing you can check in your hands which fingers feel most responsive, which are tingling the most. Knowing their relationship to different parts of your psyche will give you an insight into the area of the problem. Secondly, you can use an amplifying device such as a pendulum or dowsing rods to clarify the signals that you are picking up. In the latter case the pendulum magnifies minute, barely perceptible movements within the hand, to give a response. All dowsing techniques work on this basis. It is not the rod or pendulum that picks up information, but your body, or perhaps, to be more exact, the incoming signals are translated through your body.

Many healers feel a tingling feeling in their hands when they are sending out Ch'i. This is caused by the resonances of the healing energy passing through them. Just checking which fingers feel this sensation the most will give you an indication of how your healing is being subconsciously directed. A brief description of these correlations is given later in the chapter. Alternatively, by scanning your hands over the patient's aura different sensations will also be felt. Noting these places will indicate the position of disturbed energy in their auric field.

There is an old saying 'If your ears are burning, it is because someone is talking about you'. This reflects the idea of communicating energy between people, even at a distance. Some healers feel sensations of pain or discomfort in a similar part of their body as the problem within the person to whom they are sending healing. What is happening is that the resonating Ch'i of the patient is being broadcast back to the healer, which they then feel in their body. If you feel these sensations, check back with the person you are working with to find out if they have any problem in the corresponding area.

When giving healing you can either draw energy down through the top of your head or up through your feet. I normally start with the former. If, however, the patient has a physical illness or is very ungrounded, I will change to drawing energy up from the earth. Sometimes this happens spontaneously, which I realise because of a strong tingling sensation in my feet. If this sensation occurs when giving healing I know that I need to focus on the physical body or on helping the patient ground their energies. Check yourself where the main sensations are occurring when giving healing.

So the first level that you can use is your physical body, by being very aware of the sensations you are experiencing. Alternatively, you can develop dowsing skills which can provide valuable diagnostic information. Into this category also comes kinesiology or muscle testing techniques that can be similarly used. This latter technique is beyond the scope of this book, but courses are available for those interested.

Emotional Receptivity

The next layer of your being is your emotional body. Many people will have had the experience of being with someone and very quickly being drawn into their moods. You will also find feelings of sorrow, anger or gladness being easily invoked within when watching films. Feelings can provide a very powerful tool to help in determining underlying patterns or influences, particularly as traumas at an emotional level are some of the primary causes of certain types of physical illness. At an energetic level it relates to what is often referred to as 'gut reactions'. In my own development recognising the importance of this layer of my sensitivity was a revelation. By simply tuning into my feeling response when working with a patient I very quickly sensed underlying currents. In assessing whether I was feeling sadness, resentment, fear or whatever and where it was located in the body provided valuable clues to the problem.

Mental Receptivity

The scientific and medical worlds tend to see themselves operating at a mental level, using the rational side of their minds. This is a valid approach, providing the mind is kept open to new possibilities, even if these are in conflict with established thought. Using the rational side of ourselves to make judgements is important, and has led to the development of many beneficial systems of knowledge and technology. You need to use these faculties when assessing what is wrong with an individual. If a patient comes for treatment, carrying with them a set of hospital notes, these should not be disregarded, for they form part of the picture. Matthew Manning has said that there is no value in developing a sixth sense, when we do not use the five we already possess. Observation and listening are very important gifts to develop. There is, however, another layer to our mental body that can provide some fascinating insights. This is through clairaudience, or inner hearing, where messages are relayed to us in a verbal form.

Inner hearing or clairaudient messages can stem from contact with another spirit or being, and many healers feel that they are helped in their work by different 'healing guides'. However, these messages more generally come from aspects within and will sound like voices inside of the head. Although some people may find this prospect alarming, hearing inner voices is a natural expression of our psychic nature. It only becomes a problem, as in all things, when it is out of balance with the rest of the psyche. One of the challenges in this area is determining the source of the information. Is it coming from within or am I in contact with another spirit who is passing information to me? With a little practice it is easy to develop this gift and it can be a very useful tool as much specific information can be quickly obtained this way. It works very well with healing in that you can readily receive information while the treatment is in progress.

Another version of this level of communication is automatic writing. This is an extended form of verbal communication, where the person holds a pen or pencil over a sheet of paper and just allows the pen to write, seemingly of its own accord. The speed of the writing can sometimes be very quick, which suggests a level of access into the psyche that by-passes the logical mind. Those who practise this form of inner communication affirm that they do not think about what is being written – it just pours through them. The proof of the pudding, of course, is whether it makes sense and helps give new insights into a situation. Be open to what comes through, but always test it against your common sense. It is far better to be prudent than to believe that everything that you pick up must be 100 per cent correct. As has been said, one of the important initiations on this level is discrimination.

Healing Guides

It has long been maintained in healing circles that spirit beings will come and assist in the healing work. These are known as 'healing guides'. These spirits choose to work either with individuals or groups in helping bring forth higher levels of energy, and inspiring the healer in directing the correct balancing Ch'i to help the subject. In my experience all genuine healers will attract help from this other dimension, but you do not have to be consciously aware of these guides to be a good healer. If you feel comfortable with this idea and can start to build a level of communication with them, then this can help bring forth new insights into your work. They will always respect your 'free will' and, if thinking of other spirit guides being around causes you concern, they will not make their presence felt.

There are some schools of healing that suggest we hand over all healing to these guides. Whilst respecting this view, this is something that I would not recommend. We need to be responsible for our actions for in that we learn and grow. By all means draw upon their help, but first and foremost rely on your own higher wisdom for the healing.

Intuitive Receptivity

The final layer of your being relates to the intuitive aspect of your self which predominantly communicates through picture images. It is most closely linked to the spiritual self. It generally takes the form of an inner knowing that cannot be immediately rationalised. However, clairvoyant images are also linked to this aspect. In practice all new ideas start from this level and are then tested through the logical mind as to whether they are feasible or not. We need to develop a common-sense approach when picking any information for, to begin with, the incoming messages are like a foreign language. It is easy to misunderstand what is being communicated. This layer covers clairvoyant vision, as well as the more direct use of symbolism and metaphor.

On one occasion a trainee healer tuning into a patient had an image of a giant wood-cutting saw and then found her attention focusing on the teeth of the saw. At the end of the session she was completely perplexed at this image and at a loss to understand its meaning. Our inner consciousness will sometimes translate words into symbols, giving double meanings. In this case the 'giant saw' was actually a 'giant sore' and its teeth were the teeth of the patient. This was a fact that was unknown to the healer, but was subsequently confirmed by the patient, who had

had many operations on her teeth and gums since childhood. Learning to translate these messages can provide wonderful insights and a richness in life which is truly magical.

One simple way that this side of our consciousness can be expanded is through the use of metaphors. In these situations you can deliberately choose a symbol to represent a person or a situation and then see what happens to the metaphor. For example you could 'tune into' an individual using the symbol of a tree. Let your inner power present a picture of this tree. What type of tree is it? Is it in full leaf or not? What surrounds the tree and does it look balanced? How firm or deep are its roots? The symbolism that you get back will give you many insights into the nature of this individual and where their problems might lie.

One advantage of using metaphors is that they by-pass the logical mind, which might hold very fixed views that are at odds with the truth. We often judge things by their outer appearance and this often belies what lies beneath the surface.

It can be helpful, when using metaphors, to stick to one or two as this allows your psyche the opportunity to convey more easily its inner messages. One metaphor I use regularly is to imagine a person as a fairy-tale castle. I look at the castle and see how it is built, with what sort of materials. The moat is also important and I look at whether it is clogged with debris, or clear and flowing. The moat in the case relates to the aura. If the castle looks balanced on a physical level then I would infer that physically everything is OK. I am interested whether the drawbridge is up or down; is this an open or closed person? More fascinating still is, what is happening to the characters inside the castle? How are the king and queen getting on together? Maybe the king is hen-pecked or the queen an abused mouse.

Whatever comes up will give great insights into what needs to be worked upon to bring balance. In this case, instead of working directly on the person, I will give healing to the images and symbols of the metaphor. For example, if the queen seems downtrodden and sad, I would focus the healing to help her regain a sense of inner strength, uplift and assertiveness. I would then balance her energy with that of the king. This particular metaphor is useful in all cases of working on the sub-personalities of the patient, but if you choose to work with metaphors, you do not have to understand precisely the relationship of each aspect. By simply healing the metaphor, you will heal the corresponding part within the individual. If you perceived that a 'tree' metaphor had shallow roots, send healing to help them become deeper and firmer.

Using diagnostic techniques at this level gives many insights into the psyche of an individual. Its use should never be abused, but only ever be carried out with the inner consent of the patient to help them restore balance and wholeness. The spiritual self will only allow you to perceive what is appropriate to a situation.

It is important to realise two things in carrying out this type of diagnostic work. Firstly, you will never get the whole picture. That state perhaps is best left to God. When asking a group to 'tune into' a particular case, it is amazing how diverse, yet how relevant the answers can be. What you do perceive will give insight into what you can do to help. Secondly, whatever you pick up, no matter how irrelevant it may appear, has a connection somewhere. (Remember the lady who imagined the teeth on the wood saw?) Don't dismiss any perceptions and if necessary write them down for reference.

Before looking at specific techniques of diagnosis, there is one other fruitful area that can be explored here. This involves using divinatory systems of one form or another, like the tarot, I Ching or runes. Because of the amazing inter-connectedness of life, when we seek help in this way, the cosmos will bring forward relevant answers. I have known individuals who, faced by very difficult long-term situations, have regularly drawn the basic same set of cards. The odds against this happening with a well-shuffled pack are enormous, but it does occur. The reasons why this works can perhaps best be understood from Professor Jahn's researches demonstrating the psycho-kinetic effects of the mind (see Chapter 1). Needless to say, I recognise that the sceptics will find correlations between a set of cards and the conditions of an individual hard to take on board. Nor am I advocating dispensing with hospital doctors and replacing them with a bunch of card readers. But interestingly, some diagnostic work that I have been doing with a psychiatric doctor in one of the London hospitals has thrown up some valuable insights not available in a clinical diagnosis. As Carl Jung found, sometimes systems like the I Ching can give very perceptive answers that a more straightforward diagnosis misses. In an ideal world the two systems should work together.

Psychic Exercises

The following set of exercises is designed to help you open up your receptive abilities. They are broken down into sections to allow up to explore each aspect in turn. We start by looking at **Sensations** and follow this sequence: **Feelings; Clairaudience; Clairvoyance; Intuition**. However, you can experiment wherever you feel most drawn. There are no hard and fast rules on what should come first. It is advantageous, however, eventually to work through each section in turn. Some psychics discover a system that works for them and never try anything new. Open exploration here should be the name of the game.

Try to experiment with each section and note down your responses. If possible, work with a friend or colleague. In this way you can test each other's abilities. The time suggested is a broad guide for each exercise. This could be extended, if you wish, by working on more than one case.

Warning!

There are two points that you need to bear in mind.

1. Working with receptive psychic energy will stimulate changes within. Sometimes, like the reactivation of a rusty machine, these changes can cause temporary discomfort such as minor headaches. This is nothing to worry about, but if this occurs when you are carrying out an exercise, bring yourself back to full waking consciousness. Then carry out the rebalancing exercise given in Chapter 3.
2. Do not under any circumstances try to tune into either mentally unbalanced individuals or houses with disturbed energies. This kind of work should only be attempted by experienced healers.

These exercises have been developed for use at home or within a small group. If carried out conscientiously they will enrich your enjoyment and understanding of healing. They can also be used to increase your awareness of life and gain insights that will help you make the right decisions. We are all faced at times with critical decisions that determine our life. These decisions need to be made from a connection with the deepest part of us and not the ego mind which can often lead us astray. These exercises will greatly assist this process. Remember also that practice makes perfect. If at first you don't succeed try again another day.

Historical and Mythical Reality

Before starting the exercises, remember that one of the biggest mistakes people make when trying to gain information in this way is to mix up historical reality with mythic reality. What does this mean in practice? If in 'tuning into' an individual you saw an image of a ship travelling across a stormy sea you might conclude that this is what has happened or is going to happen to that person. If they were then to say that they have never been to sea and under no circumstances would do so, you might conclude that you were completely off beam. But, seen another way, the ship can be taken as a symbol of the self, travelling across the sea of the emotions. Asking whether the person has recently been through a stormy emotional period will most likely produce a positive reply. So, in this case the symbol was 'mythic' not 'historical'. Many psychics fall into this trap to begin with, until they understand more clearly how their inner mind works. It takes time and practice to become clearer about the way that people each pick up information. Work on the basis that whatever you sense or pick has a relevance to the situation. It might just take a little time for this to become clear.

Exercises

Preliminaries

(three minutes)

Aim: *To create the right mood before carrying out any receptive work.*

- Before you start any of these exercises carry out the **basic protection exercise** given in Chapter 4. If you are working with someone get them to put a protection around you while you are 'tuning in'. You can then do the same for them when it is their turn. Working in this way is a very good discipline and an excellent safety-first procedure.

SENSATIONS

Listening to the Messages of the Body

(five minutes)

This exercise is best carried out while sending absent healing.

- Carry out the **basic healing exercise** given in Chapter 5.
- While you are sending the healing check your own physical body and see if you have any sensations, in the hands, feet, heart area or over the top of your head. Try and describe those sensations to yourself, i.e. a tingling sensation, an itchy feeling, sensation of warmth or cold.
- Next, think more directly of your subject or recipient and see if any other sensations come forward. You might become very conscious of another part of your body.
- When you have finished disconnect, as in the standard healing procedure.
- Note down what you experienced and if possible check out your findings.

Try to repeat this exercise a number of times, noting any different sensations that you experience, particularly whether you feel energy around your hands, head or feet. If you are aware of any changes try and assess what is different about these cases.

Hand Association

I have found that there is a broad correlation between specific sensations in the hand and the area of the problem within an individual. These correlations would appear to relate to traditional palmistry interpretations. Modern scientific studies have confirmed that the shape and quality of the lines on the hand relate to certain types of illnesses and character traits. The simplest system to use at the beginning is to note which fingers appear to hold the most sensation while giving healing. There are many books on palmistry that will you a full definition, but very briefly the four fingers can be interpreted as follows:

- **Index Finger** Known traditionally as the finger of Jupiter, it relates to the ego mind and how we operate in the world, whether we are assertive or timid. It also connects to the element of fire.
- **Middle Finger** Relates to balance in the material, physical world. Known as the finger of Saturn, it also tests us, by restricting how we operate at a practical level. It has associations with money and the element of earth.
- **Ring Finger** Connects to all the emotional and creative aspects of our being. Called the finger of Apollo, the god of light and muses, it relates to the element of water.
- **Little Finger** Known as the finger of Mercury. It deals with all aspects of communication and our mental faculties. The symbol of Mercury or Hermes is the caduceus (see Chapter 6). This relates to balancing energies, especially between the masculine and feminine sides of our nature.
- **Thumb** Connects us to the higher will and the spirit within. Tingling here will indicate a problem at a spiritual level. The ball of the thumb is called the

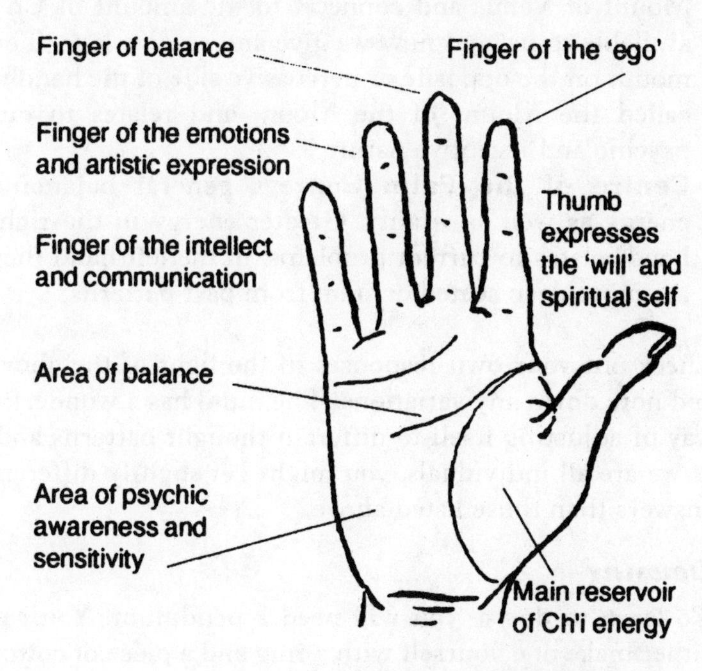

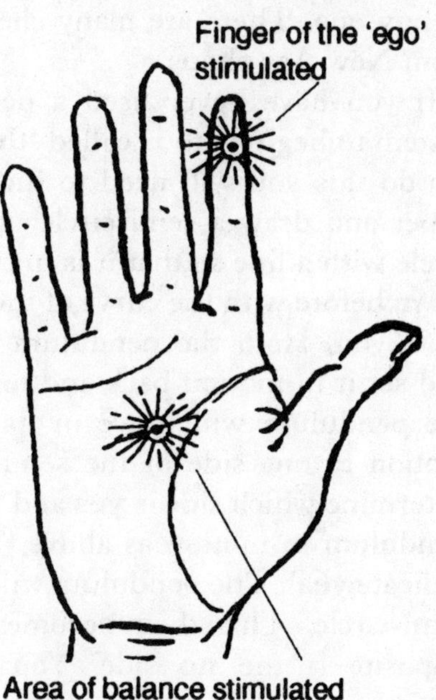

In this situation, where Ch'i is felt coming from the index finger and the centre of the palm, the indication is that the person needs to strengthen their assertiveness and also requires general balancing energy. As in reflexology, your hands and feet can give indications of areas of physical imbalance.

Mount of Venus and connects to the amount of Ch'i available to us, and how we give and receive love. The mount on the opposite or percussive side of the hand is called the Mount of the Moon, and relates to our psychic and receptive nature.

- **Centre of the Palm** Conveys general balancing energy as well as vitality. Greater energy in the right hand relates to current problems, in the left hand they are more deep seated or stem from past patterns.

Check out your own responses in the light of the above and note down any variations. The mind has a wonderful way of adjusting itself to different thought patterns and, as we are all individuals, you might get slightly different answers than those listed above.

Dowsing

To learn to dowse you will need a pendulum. You can either make one yourself with a ring and a piece of cotton or buy one. There are many cheap pendulums available from New Age shops.

If you have never used a pendulum before, a good system to begin with is called **'the protractor method'**. To do this you will need to find a piece of plain white paper and draw a semi-circle upon it. Bisect the semi-circle with a line so that it is in two halves. Set the paper down before with the curve of the semi-circle facing away from you. Hold the pendulum over the bi-secting line and set it in motion back and forwards. The idea is that the pendulum will move in its backward and forward motion to one side of the semi-circle or the other. To determine which side is **yes** and which side is **no** set your pendulum in motion as above. Then ask within 'Please indicate **yes**'. The pendulum will swing to one side of the semi-circle. This then becomes the **yes** side and the opposite is the **no** side. You can now pose **yes/no** questions to the pendulum for its answers. One of the advantages of this system is it can give variations of **yes** and **no**. If its swing stays fairly close to the centre line then the answer is qualified, in that in some cases it could be **yes** and in others **no**. If on the other hand it swings strongly to one side or the other then the answer is clear.

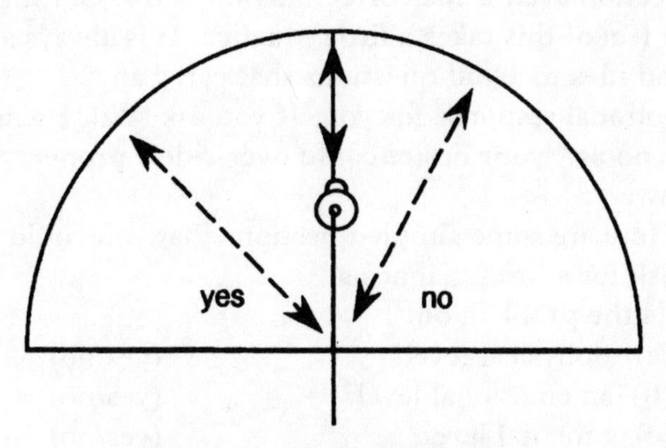

Protractor Method of Dowsing

EXERCISE

Dowsing

(twenty minutes)

Aim: *To teach the rudiments of dowsing.*

- Spend a few minutes connecting to your inner light before starting to dowse. This will ensure that your responses will be coming from the highest part of your consciousness.
- You can pose any question to the pendulum for a reply. However you must make sure that you put yourself into a meditative state and try to keep the rational side of your mind at bay. If

your thinking comes strongly into play, you will influence the movement of the pendulum. For example, if I ask a question and my logical mind affirms immediately that the answer is **yes** the pendulum is more than likely to move in that direction even if the correct answer is **no**. Getting the feel of this takes a little practice. It is always a good idea to avoid questions that carry an emotional response for you. If you ask 'Will I win the pools?' your desire could over-ride a proper answer.

- Here are some simple questions that you could ask for a brief diagnosis.

1. Is the problem on:
   (a) a physical level? (yes/no)
   (b) an emotional level? (yes/no)
   (c) a mental level? (yes/no)
   (d) a spiritual level? (yes/no)
2. Is the problem caused by:
   (a) environmental conditions? (yes/no)
   (b) genetic conditioning? (yes/no)
   (c) spiritual or past life patterns? (yes/no)

- When you have noted down the answers think of your subject and see how this appears to fit. You might like to think up other questions that can expand on this brief diagnosis. For example, if you had a **yes** for environmental conditions you could ask whether this is from the past and/or in the present. If in the present is this caused by diet or something else in the environment? So you can go on.

One word of warning. Always check when you first start using the pendulum at each session which side is **yes** and which is **no** as indicated previously. Women often find a switch in polarities during their menstrual cycles or when pregnant. Sometimes also quirky situations happen, for no apparent reason, creating a switch in the polarity of the psyche. This in turn can cause a reversal in the way that the pendulum moves.

Feelings

Your emotions provide very quick responses to energy shifts and are a valuable tool for diagnosing emotional problems. Most individuals will not openly express emotions when they come for healing, except perhaps a feeling of apprehension. So it is important to work below the surface and attune to some of the underlying patterns. These will always be reflected within your subject's energy field and so can easily be picked up.

Emotions are often classified under positive or negative headings. The former include such feelings as joy, love and happiness, while in the latter category we have sadness, fear and anger. The real problem here is that culturally we are persuaded that some emotions can be expressed and are acceptable while many others are not. This means that we can begin bottling up aspects of ourselves and this is the real cause of the problem, not the emotion itself. If people hold deep feelings of grief, anger, resentment or fear that are unacknowledged and unexpressed it will distort their energy patterns and lead in many cases to serious physical illness. For instance, researchers find links between forms of cancer and the emotions.

It can therefore be very helpful when giving healing to access into these blocked emotions and work on freeing up the underlying tension. Many healers will have had the experience of tears occurring spontaneously within their subject when the healing is being given. This is an indication of the release of emotional tension.

To access into this aspect of someone else you have to

be able to connect to your own emotions. This might, in some cases, be challenging in itself but, with a little practice, it soon becomes possible to monitor your responses. Many counsellors and therapists work on this level, and can quickly pick up minute fluctuations in their client's emotions.

EXERCISE

Feeling

(ten minutes)

Aim: *To access your feeling responses.*

- Carry out the normal procedures for giving healing either absently or with the recipient present.
- Instead of monitoring the sensations within the body, this time try and assess the underlying emotion of your client by asking within what you feel yourself, i.e. do you feel happy, sad, jealous, resentful or whatever?
- When you have pin-pointed the emotion, particularly if you sense it is blocked, feel very gently that you are allowing the patient to release this part of themselves. Allow your own inner creativity to help you with this.
- When you have completed the healing and disconnected write down your experiences.

It can sometimes take a little time to get the feel of this exercise. I found it one of the most valuable keys in my own development. As soon as I became stuck in getting visual images or obtaining clairaudient information I wold ask myself 'What do I feel from this person?' The emotional response came very quickly, either as sadness, fear or whatever and it had the effect of immediately opening up the other aspects of my receptivity. Along with the emotions would come pictures, verbal information and sensations.

The trick in all of this is when you get stuck, and we all do at times, then switch modes. Check out the other respective senses.

Clairaudience

Developing the ability to hear clairaudience information takes time and practice, although with some individuals it comes very easily. We have seen that the information we hear can either come from your own higher consciousness or it can be relayed by a guide or other spiritual presence. The problem with this latter category is that people can occasionally open themselves up to all sorts of influences, some of them not good. It is therefore essential to take precautions to ensure that this does not happen. Indeed to begin with it is much better not to try and connect with any guide, but to work only on accessing your own inner wisdom.

To do this you will need to start observing your thinking process and to sense that you can separate out the different parts of your psyche. In other words you need to recognise the part of your mind that can independently monitor what another part is doing. This is standard procedure in some meditation schools. The first thing you will need to establish is whether you think more in pictures or in words. Look at something in the room, then close your eyes and try and recall what you were looking at. Do you see a picture of the object or are you aware of words describing what you were seeing? It will often be a mixture of both. Now imagine you are going to describe to someone else what it was that you saw. What are the processes that are going on in your mind? How much is visual and how much linguistic?

With a little practice it becomes possible to 'hear' yourself thinking about things. Language is an amazing development in that it provides us with a means of communicating logical ideas and passing on information. Yet despite this the majority of communication within human beings, about 60 per cent, takes a non-verbal form. So there must be other parts of us that can respond to information from many different levels. By learning to observe your thinking process and 'hear' the words that are coming into your head you can start to create a link with the messages from your own spiritual self. You can practise this in conjunction with healing or more broadly by gaining information about all sorts of things in life. There may be problems that have cropped up in your life, which require some form of action. You can learn to attune within to get the correct insight or information on what you need to do to solve them.

EXERCISE

Clairaudience

(ten minutes)

***Aim**: To connect linguistically to your inner wisdom.*

- Bring to mind some question or problem within your life that you would like some insight about.
- Carry out the **body awareness exercise**.
- Carry out the exercise for connecting with your own inner light.
- Put a protection around yourself.
- Pose the question in your mind and imagine that the deeper part within is communicating information to you. Try and be aware of the verbal messages that are being relayed. Note down whatever you pick up and see whether it

makes sense. Even if totally bizarre comments appear to come through try not to dismiss them out of hand but consider them.

- When you have gained as much as you feel you can, bring yourself back to full waking consciousness and ground yourself.
- Try to keep a diary to begin with of the questions that you asked and the replies that came through.

Messages to be wary of

There are certain types of messages that you need to be on your guard against. These can be listed under three simple headings:

- ego inflationary;
- inciting intolerance;
- fear inducing.

Indeed, these three headings can guide you whatever teaching, philosophy or spiritual message that you hear. Perhaps added to the above you could include whether the teaching encourages free thought or not. Be wary of those that do not.

Ego inflationary messages usually take the form of encouraging you believe that you are a very special person, even the reincarnation of a famous individual from history and that you have an important mission on earth. This can also apply to groups. Do not fall into the trap of believing such statements. They are not true in the sense that they are given and will only lead you up the garden path. Everybody is unique and we all have important missions. Such information can sometimes come forward to check whether we have learnt the lesson of humility and discernment.

The messages that encourage intolerance can be very subtle. They usually take the form of suggesting that certain individuals or groups are undesirable in some form or another and should be shunned. One of the wisest comments I ever heard from a channelled source was that 'Evil is only evil as long as it is rejected'. We can never grow spiritually while we condemn others. All criticism is actually self-criticism if we did but know it. This is not to say that we should become doormats to malicious or destructive individuals. Our freedoms need to be defended rigorously. If we were to see a man or woman with a large stick thrashing a child the first step must be to take away the stick and restrain the person. However, we also need to try and understand that person and help them move away from needing to act in that way again.

Fear-inducing messages, of the kind encouraged by certain religious doctrines, suggest that if you do not toe the party line or believe certain things then dire consequences will follow. It is better to ignore all messages that encourage this fear element. Believe those things that support freedom of choice and encouragement for you to grow in the manner best suited to yourself.

The above information is important as there is a plethora of advice coming through from channelled sources. Some of it is excellent, but some leaves a lot to be desired. If you apply these simple rules to everything you hear or read you will not go far wrong in judging whether it is worthy of attention.

Clairvoyance

To work with the clairvoyant side of your consciousness you will need to develop the visual imagery side of your mind. Many individuals find this difficult, to the extent that some appear not to be able to visualise at all. What is important is not necessarily to see an image in pristine clarity but to have a sense of what is there. If you are unsure you can easily test this out for yourself. Carry out the following exercise:

EXERCISE

Clairvoyance

(five to ten minutes)

***Aim**: To develop inner vision.*

- Close your eyes and imagine a tree in as much detail as you can. Then answer the following questions.
  What sort of tree came to mind?
  Was it a big or little tree?
  Was it a deciduous tree or an evergreen?
  Was it in full leaf or bare?

If you can answer these questions, even if you did not clearly 'see' the tree, your imagery mind is up to the task. If not you will need to practise. There are many visualisation tapes available on the market that can help you develop this imagery sense.

Clairvoyant images can come in two forms. They can provide factual information and symbolic or mythic information. It is very important to determine which is which. You will only find this out by getting plenty of feedback. If the answers that come back do not appear to have any connection with the person, note them down and think about them later. You might suddenly then get a new insight. It is more difficult to interpret symbolic information and this requires quite a bit of practice. Those colleagues who I know have spent time on this have found it enormously worthwhile. You will need a reference book to look up the traditional meaning of symbols. See the Bibliography at the end of this book for a suitable one.

The simplest way to develop this side of your mind is to work with metaphors. The following exercise will show you how to do this:

EXERCISE

Metaphor

(five to ten minutes)

***Aim**: To develop the ability to work with symbols at an intuitive level.*

- Think of someone who needs help.
- Carry out your **body awareness exercise** and put up your protection.
- Attune to your inner light, your higher wisdom.
- In thinking of the person imagine them as a car.
- What sort of car do you see?
- Does the car look as though it needs physical repairs? If so, where?
- What sort of location is the car being driven in? Is it moving forward or stuck in a traffic jam?
- Who is driving the car and are there other passengers with them?
- How are the people in the car getting on?

Write down your answers and then relate them back to your subject. For example, if the headlights of the car seemed damaged does this mean there is something wrong with their eyesight? Or perhaps their inner vision, the way that they look at life, needs attention? Think about all the symbolism you perceived. Each part contains a message. In reflecting on this metaphor, what insights have you gained?

There are many metaphors that can be used, such as houses, gardens, trees, landscapes etc. With practice you can soon learn to allow your inner knowing to bring forward what is appropriate for the particular situation.

Ideally you should learn to combine all the systems that have been covered here so that you move between them with ease.

Problem Solving

The above exercises can be adapted to help solve problems whether they are to do with work, friends or family. We all have the ability to open up to the part of us that has a deep awareness of our situation, and what needs to be brought forth to help us feel fulfilled and joyful. Developing your receptive yin aspect will further this process.

In addition to all of the inner mental exercises included here, there are many other external systems for gaining insights into problems, life patterns or the causes of illness. These involve the use of different divinatory systems such as the I Ching, runes, tarot, Medicine Cards etc. The principle behind the way in which such systems work is based upon what Jung called 'synchronicity'. In other words by drawing certain cards whilst thinking of, or attuning to, a specific problem, the higher aspects of your consciousness will select the appropriate cards, or whatever, that can give an insight into the situation. From my own experience these different systems can give a very perceptive overview on the underlying dynamics of any problem or life pattern.

There are at present an enormous number of different systems available and more are coming on to the market all the time. Some of these systems, like the I Ching, are of ancient origin dating back at least 3,000 years. Others, like the Medicine Cards, are modern inventions based upon an individual's creative insight. Using one or other of these systems can provide a valuable extra tool in helping the development of your psychic faculty. If you wish to have fun exploring one or other of these different techniques allow your intuition to draw you to the system that is most appropriate for you at this moment in time.

To help unlock a solution to a specific problem the following ritual can be carried out.

EXERCISE

Problem-Solving Ritual

(five to ten minutes)

***Aim**: To unlock the deeper aspects of the spiritual self to solve problems.*

- Light a candle and sit quietly for a few moments thinking about the problem.
- Carry out the **body awareness exercise** then attune to your light within.
- Think of the problem and if possible see it in symbolic form. (For example if the problem is around money, you could imagine gold coins, £5 notes or something similar.)
- Next imagine a gold triangle and place the symbolic image with your question into the middle of the triangle.
- Offer the triangle out to the cosmos with a strong request for help, understanding and the resolving of your problem.

In one form or another the answer should come back to you within three days.

Summary

- Energy can either flow into us or away from us. In Ancient China this was known in terms of yin energy or yang energy.
- Sending healing is an aspect of yang energy. Picking up information psychically is an aspect of yin energy.
- As healers we need to develop both polarities.
- There are four generally recognised layers to our being. These are the physical, emotional, mental and spiritual aspects that correlate to the four elements of earth, water, air and fire respectively.
- These four elements also correspond to four aspects of our personality: sensation, feeling, thinking and intuition.
- Each aspect can be used independently or collectively to pick up information at a psychic level.

Further Study

Those interested in further exploration and study in this area should read my book *Develop Your Intuition and Psychic Powers* (Bloomsbury, 1996) which contains many more exercises.

CHAPTER 9

Chakras – Keys To Healing?

Be still
And discover your centre of peace

(TAO 16)

The Tradition of the Chakras

The concept of the chakras is an integral part of Hindu and Yogic tradition and has over recent years been widely accepted as part of the new paradigms of Western belief. The chakras stem from a very ancient body of knowledge which sought to understand the energetic balance of our being. They are used as key balancing points within us and their role in the healing field, both for balancing our own energies and those of someone else, is widely acknowledged.

Over the past few years much new material has been written about chakras, so that today we have an accumulation of knowledge that seems definitive. The difficulty with this is that many authors have worked from a series of assumptions, some of which are suspect. As Larry LeShan has stated we need to challenge our beliefs continually to arrive at the truth. Each step of the way must be rigorously checked. An example of this is the now almost universally accepted association of a specific colour with each chakric centre. This is based on the colours of the rainbow and connects red to the base chakra and violet with the crown.

Because of this most healers and students of yoga, for example, will tell you that green is the colour of the heart chakra. However, in my experience over many years working with all sorts of people tuning into their own chakras, these colour associations do not necessarily apply. What actually happens is that people will present their own pattern of colour. So for the heart chakra many different colours have come forward, across the whole range, including gold and white. The most general are blue, pink, red, gold and green; probably in that order. It may surprise readers to know that this colour association with the spectrum is a very recent addition to chakric knowledge. It was certainly not part of the Vedic traditions, from where the concept of the chakras originated. Nor was it confirmed by the early research work on chakras carried out by C.W. Leadbeater from the Theosophical Society. According to his extensive research green was associated with the solar plexus centre and gold with the heart.

There is nothing wrong with additions to traditional knowledge as long as they can be validated in practical ways. In this chapter I will attempt to present a slightly different picture of the chakras. I realise that in flying in the face of current thinking I run the risk of offending some. However I believe that it is important to question our present understanding on this tantalising subject. To do this, we need to look at how chakras were traditionally understood.

The word chakra comes from the Sanskrit, where it literally means 'a wheel'. The word, however, carries an implication of movement, so a more exact translation would be a 'moving wheel' or 'spinning wheel'. The

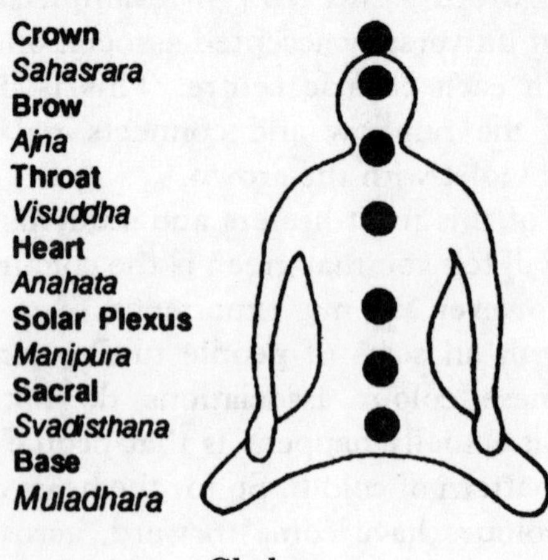

Chakras

chakric centres, traditionally seven in number, were seen as vortices of energy, on the front of a human body (as illustrated). Each chakra was perceived as carrying a particular quality or flavour of energy through to the physical. Each chakra was associated with a Hindu deity, a god or goddess, and each had its own sound, geometric pattern and colour association (although not the colours we use today). The chakra at the base of the spine (*muladhara*) was seen as representing the most physical aspect of our being, while that on the top of the head (*sahasrara*) was the most spiritual. These chakras were also seen as being linked together by channels of energy called *nadis*. The chakras contain three specific elements. They are:

- energy centres for giving and receiving Ch'i;
- each linked to a particular spiritual quality;
- located at generally recognised specific places on the physical body.

This latter statement needs to be qualified. Most schools

today, and in the past, show the chakras in a straight line commencing at the base of the spine and rising to the top of the head. C. W. Leadbeater located the solar plexus centre over the spleen, and therefore to the right of the body seen from the front. I have seen drawings of the chakras from Nepal and Rajasthan with the base chakra starting in the area of the knees. This may be artistic licence but bears out that variation that can found. The best test from my own experience is to look to those places where we feel energy movement at a sensation level within the body.

Energy Centres in the Body

Many individuals, when working psychically, through healing or some other clairvoyant activity, are aware of Ch'i stimulation in different parts of themselves. Novice healers when they first start are often aware of a warmth or tingling in their hands. With practice you can soon learn to discern other places, including the feet, brow, heart and the crown of the head. Also, when you experience strong emotions some areas stand out more than others; a churning in the pit of the stomach, an aching heart and a choking feeling in the throat are quite common. When sexually aroused we are also aware of a specific location of that energy within the body.

By noting down these locations an area of objective assessment can be reached on where you experience different energies within you. The level of energy closest to the physical body is known as the etheric body. It is generally acknowledged in healing circles that the changes in the energy of this body directly cause shifts at a physical level. This ties in with the concept of resonance where if the physical body corresponds to the base octave of the piano, then the etheric is the next octave up. The chakras then, in part at least, must be energy centres in the etheric body. This is confirmed by a number of writers, notably C. W. Leadbeater and David Tansley.

The Spirit/Body Link

Stepping Down in Density

Let us now move away from the chakras and go back to the original symbolism of the link between the spiritual self or soul and the physical body. We have seen that there is a gradual step down of energy between these two aspects of our being. This stepping down in density can be symbolically seen in the same way as we perceive the gradual shift of colour through the spectrum. If you look closely through a prism, into a rainbow or at a CD you will see this movement as one colour gently merges with the next. There are no hard and fast borders, and closer scrutiny will reveal many more shades of colour than the seven that we normally accept. In a similar way, the energy from the spiritual self gradually steps down in density until it meets the physical. However, like colour it has been helpful to understand this stepping down process by grouping these shifts into neat packages. When Newton first classified the seven colours of the spectrum, he did so because he was coming from an esoteric stand-point. Seven was a sacred number and therefore seemed appropriate. He could equally have divided the spectrum into 8, 12 or as many colours as he liked. Seven seemed about right and it has stuck.

Patterns of Energy

In esoteric tradition it was also realised that the known universe was held together by certain principle energies. Science is aware of many of these forces at a physical level, but there are many spectrums beyond dense matter.

These powers permeate the collective unconscious of humanity. In order to make them more real and comprehend their quality, most cultures have clothed them in the garb of their different gods and goddesses. In Taoist belief, these principles are reflected in the eight tri-grams of the I Ching. In Christianity they have been grafted on to key personages of the Christian story as well as the archangels, like Raphael and Gabriel. By reading across mythologies we can gain an amazing insight into the working of these forces. This is a vast subject, with many overlaps, but one that can be immensely rewarding. We can better understand this principle by using our colour spectrum as a model. Let us imagine the generative force of the universe, whether we call this God, Allah or whatever, as a white light. This moves out from the source and hits the spectrum of the cosmos, so splitting into a myriad of colours. Within each colour there is a facet of the whole and each represents a different spiritual principle, such as love, truth, balance, creativity and so on.

Certain patterns of this energy have been more dominant in the formation of planet earth and the spiritual leaders of all cultures have appreciated this. This is why, when we scrape beneath the surface of all the major religions, there is a very similar message to be found. To understand these principles and simplify them to a certain extent some cultures have chosen to work with 7 main energies, others like the Ancient Chinese with 8, and others still like Christianity and the Ancient Greeks with 12. It does not really matter how many we choose. As these are universal principles, like the DNA molecule within us, they will appear within every aspect and atom of whom and what we are. Each chakra also contains the energies of every other chakra. Yet under the law of correspondences, they will also have specific connections with a part of the physical body. Most people for example would identify a feeling of love with the heart. Our language, with terms like heart-throb, broken hearted, heart-stopping and heart-warming supports this notion as does the proliferation of heart-shaped cards on Valentine's Day.

We could therefore choose a set number of principles and relate them to different aspects of the physical body and the energy fields that surround us. This is precisely what the Hindu sages tried to do with the concept of the chakras. They also built into the system the notion that there is a graduation of density energy between the physical body and the spirit. This they symbolised by the concept of the movement of energies from the base to the crown. There was also a reason culturally why this idea was very relevant at the time when these ideas were first formalised.

As has been said, because these are universal principles, like the hologram, they will be found in everything. Every part of us reflects these energies. This is why a reflexologist working on the feet can, for example, effect a shift in energy in the liver. There is a correspondent connection. The chakric system, as originally propounded, was based upon empirical insight. It arose from the need of the culture at the time for a model of how the spiritual forces worked within both men and women. What we should now question is whether that model is still appropriate and if not in what way should it be revised.

I find it very interesting working with many different people and posing the question 'Where do you see your spiritual self residing in relation to your body?' Think back to when you carried out this exercise in the chapter on meditation. Few people actually see this as being focused in a space over the top of their head. Most common, interestingly, is the heart, but other places include the head, solar plexus, sacral or hara centres, as well as enveloping themselves. This also makes sense for a very good reason.

Part of esoteric tradition is that on each incarnation we will deliberately choose to work with a specific group of spiritual energies or principles. In Alice Bailey's teachings these are referred to as the seven rays, and the concept suggests that we will elect to manifest ray one, two or whatever as part of our life pattern. In yoga tradition this principle is also present. The word yoga means 'union' and the aim is to find union with the spiritual self. There are a number of different schools of yoga. Bhakti yoga is based on love and devotion, Raja yoga espouses wisdom and meditation, Karma yoga encourages good works, Gnana yoga occurs through discernment and the balance of opposites, Hatha yoga develops union through the body, Kundalini yoga awakens the psychic spiritual energies from within and Laya Yoga is based on balancing the energies of the chakras. Each system can be seen as the manifestation of a different spiritual principle and therefore coming under a different ray.

When we tune into ourselves to locate the essence of our spiritual being, we will most likely connect it to the place within, that most clearly resonates with the principles we are working with in this life. Therefore the first adaptation I would like to see brought forward in an understanding of the chakras is to move away from thinking of the crown chakra as the most spiritual part of our being. Each chakra reflects a spiritual quality and each is important to the whole. Where you choose to put your emphasis shows your uniqueness as an individual and honours your developmental needs. This accords broadly with Taoist belief which saw different aspects of the 'spirit' associated with the organs of the liver, heart, spleen, lungs and kidneys.

How Many Chakras?

We also need to consider whether it is appropriate to work with seven chakras, eight chakras or whatever. As has been said this is a somewhat arbitrary choice, for like the colours of the rainbow there could be an infinite range of colours to choose from. The most powerful resonant numbers within the cultural traditions of this planet are 7, 8 and 12. My preference would be to stick with one of these numbers.

Balancing the Chakras

The chakric centres are located over specific parts of the body and are part of our etheric self. Their function is to act as an energy exchange point, allowing Ch'i to enter and leave. Because they also link with spiritual principles, each chakra has to be connected out to all layers of who and what we are. Energetically then we can see the chakras as gateways to Ch'i, moving from the spiritual to the physical and back to the spiritual again. Another way of looking at it would be to say that each layer of our being has its set of chakric centres. Metaphorically, we could imagine that each chakra is a different instrument within an orchestra that is us. Our spiritual self, as the conductor, attempts to keep the orchestra playing together and in tune. If any part starts to play off key or out of step then problems will occur. Sending healing and balance to specific chakras that are off rhythm or playing discordantly can bring the orchestra back into harmony once more. This is why balancing the chakras has become a very important part of the present understanding of healing.

In approaching healing in this way we are accessing the very core structure of whom and what we are. Therefore this approach needs to be carried out with a great deal of care and consideration. Imagine your orchestra is playing a piece of Beethoven. Along comes the healer and sits in the audience watching and listening carefully. The music seems fine but suddenly the healer notices that the woodwind section is not playing. Not knowing this particular piece of music they conclude that something must be wrong and without reference to the conductor the healer takes steps to get this section up and playing once more. This causes upset to the balance of the whole piece of music and disruption within the orchestra for had they but waited, or known the piece of music, they would have realised that the woodwind section were not due to play for several more bars.

This might seem like an extreme case, but unfortunately I have seen it happen before and no doubt will see it happen again. When any healing is given it must be done in conjunction with the conductor of the orchestra, the spiritual self. We must be very cautious of making specific judgements on the state of balance of an individual's chakric system. Healers will make assessments that one or other chakra is not functioning correctly because they do not sense its energy very strongly. But, like the analogy above, each chakra has a specific role to fulfil within the life plan of an individual. This means that not all chakras are fully active all the time. Until, as a healer, you have developed the necessary spiritual and psychic awareness to work directly on the chakras, it is much better to only think of balancing these centres. Healing this level in a specific way requires many years of experience. The other trap that healers can sometimes fall into is diagnosing the chakras only at an etheric level. The energies that we sense on the front of the body are those closest to the physical. We might be aware that at this level the energy is not very strong, but at other levels, the emotional or mental, it may be functioning quite adequately. To be fully cognisant of specific chakric imbalances requires detailed inner vision or awareness.

The Chakric Centres

In order not to complicate matters further, I will stick to the traditional seven chakras when looking at their role and function. The one addition to the list is the feet. This may seem surprising, but this centre has a specific role in relation to healing and helps us access energy from the earth. But first we will look at the seven known major chakras.

The information I give about these centres is drawn from my own experiences and the many students I have worked with. Not all the time does the information given below conform to present beliefs. If it stimulates thought and assists you in understanding this fascinating subject then I am content.

Muladhara or Base Chakra

Located at the base of the spine, this centre is traditionally seen as connecting us with the earth and all the basic instinctual functions of our being. In Hindu belief it was ruled over by the deities Brahma and Dakini, and was symbolised by the elephant. Brahma was the supreme creative god and therefore this chakric centre connects us to all aspects of our creativity. At a physical level this is associated with sexual activity but any aspect of creativity, from the masterpieces of Leonardo, to the building of the Taj Mahal is an aspect of this energy. Tantric tradition is based on drawing sexual energy up through the different centres to allow this creativity to flow through all parts of whom and what we are. Many specific practices were developed to achieve this movement, but it is not necessary to go to such lengths. By fully acknowledging the energy of this centre within us, it will allow its expression to flow in our lives.

The chakra is symbolised by a four-leafed lotus, and

both Brahma and Dakini hold four objects in their hands. This represents the four elements and how the energy of this centre interweaves with the basic forces of nature. It is interesting to note that poltergeist activity is most commonly associated with children moving into puberty, when the energies of this centre are being awoken. An unconscious release of this energy causes physical objects to move.

The Kundalini serpent, containing the twin polarity energies of Shakti and Shiva, is found here. Its release, to illuminate our higher consciousness, was part of the initiatic practices of the Yogis.

The symbol of the elephant is also found here. It represents the story of Maya, the mother of Buddha, who dreamed that her son entered her womb in the form of a white elephant causing his conception.

Individuals are most aware of the energy of this centre during sexual relationships. The stimulation that comes when we are in the presence of highly sexual people is a good example of this resonant connection at work. This energy is also used within many traditions for spiritual practices. By blocking its physical expression, the object is to raise its energies to higher levels of awareness. Magical practices using sexual release work in a slightly different way. The aim here is to bring about changes in and

Traditional symbolism for the base chakra

domination over the physical world in which we reside.

Many current schools of thought associate this chakra with the adrenal glands, the basic flight and fight mechanism of the body, and not with sexual energy. I am not so sure about this and prefer, for the reasons given above, to connect this energy with the reproductive glands.

Svadisthana or Sacral Centre

This chakra is located just below the navel. Its symbol is the upturned crescent, within a six-petalled lotus that like the chalice receives the waters of life. It is associated with the Hindu god Vishnu and his consort Rakini. The name Svadisthana means 'sweetness', and carries an idea of harmony and balance. It is one and the same as the hara centre, used in Shiatsu massage, and Chinese and Japanese martial arts. Hara is the key physical balancing point of the body, our centre of gravity and the fulcrum of whom and what we are. All physical actions and spiritual disciplines should stem from the hara. It also carries an energy of nurture, holding the developing foetus within its orbit. Its animal symbol is the fish, which swims in the waters of the emotions. Its link with water connects it at an energetic level with the kidneys and the elimination of unwanted energies from the body.

Vishnu, one of the great triad of gods that includes Brahma and Shiva, was one of the supreme gods of the Hindu pantheon. His name means to pervade, and he portrayed the quality of preservation and protection. Whenever humankind was threatened by evil Vishnu assumed a different guise to protect the world. His most famous incarnation for the Hindus was as Krishna, but the Brahmins also associated him with the Buddha.

The energy of this centre also connects us strongly into our psychic nature, particularly, the receptive mediumistic qualities of our consciousness. Because of this it has an association with alcohol, drugs and meditation. One of Vishnu's symbols is the lotus on which the Buddha resides. It is interesting to note also that the Ancient Chinese sages saw this centre as the seat of consciousness.

Manipura or Solar Plexus Centre

This chakra carries all the vitality we associate with the element of fire. Symbolised by the ten-petalled lotus its animal symbol, the ram, is connected with the Hindu god of fire, Agni. Like the Western astrological association with Aries and the planet Mars, this centre is the main focus of our physical vitality and drive. It connects with all strong emotions, including anger, fear and passion. It therefore also has an association with adrenalin, and the flight and fight mechanisms of the body. When its energies are depleted we feel tired and run down. When active we have an enormous energetic capacity.

The word Manipura means 'gem centre' or the 'jewel in the lotus'. It is ruled by Rudra and Lakini. Rudra was the god of storms and was associated with the destructive aspects of Agni. This warns us of the potential damaging qualities that can come from this centre if its energies are not balanced. In consequence many people feel frightened of its energy and block its free expression. It relates to the digestive system which provides us with the necessary vitality of the body. It is the chakra most likely to be affected in all cases where we lack drive. It is also seen as the centre connecting with our 'ego' consciousness and how we project ourselves into the world.

Anahata or Heart Chakra

The word Anahata means 'unstruck'. It relates to all aspects connected with the qualities of love, compassion and transformation. Its animal symbol is the antelope, a form of deer, that connects us with a feeling of gentleness and sensitivity. It links with the physical heart and the lungs and was traditionally associated with the element of air. Within the 12-petalled lotus is the hexagram indicating the unification of the downward forces of creation with the upward forces of consciousness.

Its presiding deities are Isa and Kakini. One of the lesser-known gods of the Hindu pantheon, Isa is lord of speech, he grants boons and dispels fear. The Ancient Egyptian goddess Isis can also be associated with this centre. She was a goddess of magic and inner wisdom, and helps connect us to the world beyond the physical, ruled over by Osiris. Over her heart area sits the sacred knot of Isis which, like the girdle of Aphrodite, can protect us from all ills.

The energy from this chakra has often been connected with the thymus centre, a little understood endocrine gland that is now thought to relate to our immune system. The heart chakra is considered by some to be the presiding chakric impulse of the Aquarian Age, moving us away from the more emotional energies of the solar plexus centre, that dominated the Piscean epoch. These solar 'ages' are based upon an astronomical event known

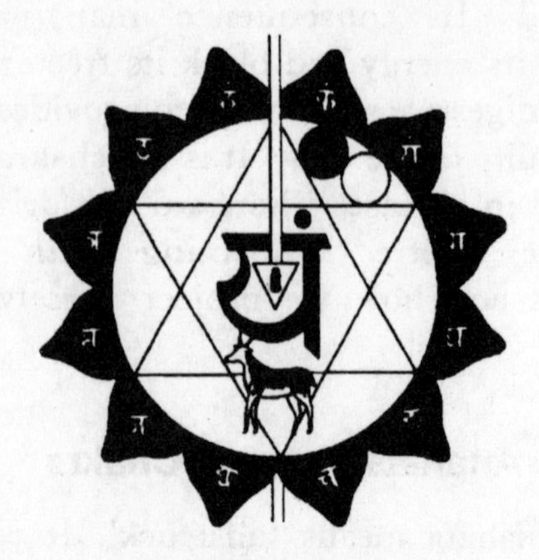

Traditional symbolism for the heart chakra

as the precession of the equinoxes, which takes the sun through all the signs of the zodiac roughly every 26,000 years. Dividing this by the twelve signs gives an approximate time span of 2,160 years for each sign of the zodiac. Many esotericists believe that the start of the Piscean Age commenced within a hundred years before the birth of Christ and that we are now moving into the 'New Age' energies of Aquarius. The spiritual expression of this 'heart chakra' energy is best exemplified by the work of St Francis of Assisi.

Visuddha or Throat Chakra

Located over the throat like its physical organ, the Visuddha chakra is connected to all aspects of communication. Visuddha means 'pure' or 'to purify', and also links to artistic appreciation and awareness, and hence has a connection with creativity. Sounds that emerge from the throat can be used to communicate information and to express emotions. Sound is one of the most potent forces and reminds us of St John's statement 'In the beginning was the word. Music and sound can weave together to bring about altered states of consciousness and illumination. Communication relates not just to the physical world but between worlds, linking us to higher states of consciousness. Telepathic communication and channelling are aspects of this centre.

One of the most powerful expressions of this chakra is through mantras and chanting. The resonance created by the sounds produced can affect each of the chakras, stimulating and balancing their energies. This is a very specific 'science' and needs to be taught by a qualified master.

The chakra is ruled over by Sadasiva and Sakini, two deities that are really aspects of Shiva. The symbol of this centre is a white elephant, an aspect of Indra who rides a golden chariot drawn by two steeds, which is sometimes seen as an aspect of the sun. This has a link with the Greek Apollo, the god of light, beauty and intellectual prowess. This chakra is similarly associated with music, poetry, the mind and prophecy. At a physical level it connects to the thyroid glands.

Ajna or Brow Chakra

Located at a point just above and between the eyes, the name of this chakra means 'to command' or 'to know'. This is the traditional 'third eye' chakra that makes us aware of other dimensions and realms of consciousness. The word command gives insight into this chakra's ability to balance and control the other chakric centres. It relates to all aspects of intuition and inner knowing, and is an important chakric energy in healing.

Its symbol is a two-petalled lotus, that spreads our like two wings. This indicates the balance of opposites and the ability of the mind to soar into higher states of consciousness. It reminds us of the winged solar disk of the Ancient Egyptians, a symbol of initiation into the inner mysteries. It also symbolises the two hemispheres of the brain and their specific functions.

Paramasiva, the residing deity, was both male and female, representing the balance of opposites that can be achieved when the energies of this centre are harnessed.

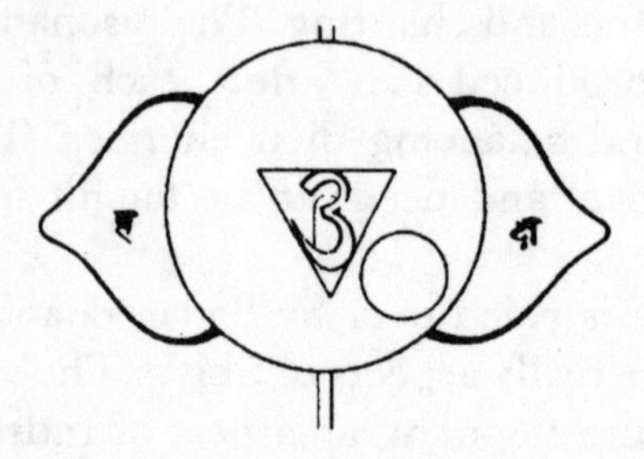

Traditional symbolism for the brow chakra

In Greek mythology the great goddess Athene, bright eyed and brandishing a spear, sprang fully armed from the brow of Zeus, indicating her link with the energies of this centre. Athene symbolised wisdom, and she played an important role in protecting and aiding heroes on their journeys. Some schools of thought ascribe the pineal gland to this centre while for others it is the pituitary. There are good arguments for both. The pituitary gland is the main control gland of the body and would therefore seem to equate with the name of this chakra. However the pineal responds to light sensitivity in the brow area and its little known functions could connect to higher levels of awareness.

Sahasrara or Crown Chakra

Located on the crown of the head, like the tonsure of a medieval monk, this chakra is said to link us with the spiritual self. The name means 'thousandfold' which refers to the number of petals of the lotus associated with this centre. It was seen as the seat of the Hindu god Shiva, the destroyer. His destructiveness aims at breaking down illusion, but also reflects the perennial battle between the light and dark sides of our nature. In Ancient Egyptian mythology the great ruling god was Osiris, who brought forward all the benefits of civilisation. But he was overthrown by his evil brother Set, who gained control of Osiris's kingdom and preceded to rule it for his own nefarious purposes. This tells us that it is through our minds that evil can enter our consciousness and pervert our spiritual nature. The Buddha said 'Of all the sins of the world the greatest is the sin of mindlessness'. It is this quality that allows humanity to perpetrate some of the many abuses that are inflicted within our species and against the planet itself.

After he is slain, Osiris is resurrected by Isis (love) and then proceeds to rule from a world beyond the physical.

This indicates that we need to work consciously on linking or grounding the energies of this chakra within ourselves. Its qualities relate to philosophy, rulership, healing and cosmic principles. It reflects the 'Christ' principle with us.

In Yogic tradition the aspirant would try to unite the energies of Shiva and Shakti, representing the uniting of the physical and spiritual, masculine and feminine elements of the psyche. This should still be our goal, but we do not now need to see this in the restrictive concept of uniting the energies of the crown with the base chakra.

Feet Chakra

The feet chakra had a relatively minor role in Vedic tradition, although I include it here because of its relationship with healing. The energy of this chakra is activated in reflexology and metamorphic technique. It most directly connects us to the energy of the earth and acts as a transformer for these energies, both back and forward. Each foot acts as part of the polarity balance of this chakra, it is not that there is a different chakra in each foot.

Because of the connection with the earth, that brought us forth, this chakra links us back to our roots, both spiritually and genetically. Its energies can be used to balance the feminine and masculine principles within, and are particularly useful in helping us ground the spiritual aspects within the physical vehicle.

Many healers will feel the energies coming through this chakra when they are giving healing, particularly to physical conditions.

EXERCISE

Balancing the Chakras

(five to ten minutes)

***Aim**: To balance the energies of the chakric centres.*

- This exercise can be used either for self-healing (balancing one's own chakras) or for healing others. It will be given in the self-healing form here, but the principles can be easily applied when giving healing.
- Adopt your usual meditative posture, close your eyes and link with the light within, your spiritual self.
- Connect with the chakra that most closely relates to the position where you sense your inner light is located.
- Ask within for a symbol of balance (if none comes forward use the equidistant cross in the circle) and place it over the chakra. Feel it is balancing the energies.
- Next imagine that the chakra is breathing, opening and closing very gently, like a flower.* Repeat this three or four times, before coming back to seeing it balanced once more.
- Now move on to another chakra. Allow your intuition to decide which is the next chakric centre to work upon and repeat the process given above.
- When you have completed working in this way on all the chakras, feel the connecting link of energy between them, both from crown to feet and back again.

- Finally, bring yourself back to full conscious awareness.

***Note:** It is important when working on others as part of the healing, that you do not force these chakras open. All that is necessary is to have the sense that they are gently breathing, in and out, in a balanced way.

Healing the Chakric Centres

To send balancing healing to the chakric centres apply the normal healing techniques. You can in addition place your hands over each chakra in turn to send this balancing thought. Many healers will stand to one side of their subject and hold either their left or right hand from 4 to 6 in from the body over each chakra in turn. The other hand is held in a corresponding position over the spine. It does not really matter whether you start at the crown, base or some intermediate position, as long as you work on balancing all the chakras. Complete the exercise by sending a balancing thought to the link between the spirit and the body. In fact, when you send healing to the auric energies, you are achieving the same ends. Balance the aura and you balance the chakras.

We can use the chakras as gateways to higher states of consciousness, as well as healing aspects of ourselves that are blocked within these centres. The following exercise can help with this, but a word of warning. If possible carry out this exercise with another individual present who can help you balance and integrate what you experience. If you start to experience any difficulties bring yourself back to full waking consciousness.

The following exercise is a way of exploring the

spiritual qualities that lie within each chakric centre. This exercise can be carried out, linking to different chakric centres, over a period of time. It is advisable not to attempt to explore more than one chakric centre per week as you will need to allow adequate time to assimilate your experiences. Try to keep a record of what happens so that you can plot your progress in understanding the different qualities of your chakric energies.

ADDITIONAL EXERCISE

(five to ten minutes)

Aim: *To access into the spiritual energy of each chakra.*

- Adopt your normal meditative pose, close your eyes and link with your light within the spiritual self.
- Next think of the chakra that you wish to link with and imagine it as a flower that is gently opening.
- Project your mind into the centre of the flower, feeling into its essence and allowing yourself to experience any other images or impressions that come to mind.
- When you have completed this, send a thought of balance to the centre.
- Bring yourself back to full waking consciousness.

Summary

- The word chakra means 'spinning wheel' and indicates an energy vortex over the physical body.
- The chakras have three specific aspects – they both give and receive energy across all the spectrum, they are linked to a specific spiritual quality, in the physical world they have a specific location within the body.
- The traditional number of chakras is seven. Other schools add more and this is perfectly valid. There is no set number.
- As each chakra has its spiritual aspect it is incorrect to see the crown chakra as the seat of our spirituality. This is only valid in a symbolic sense.
- Healing the chakras needs to be carried out with a great deal of care. Working directly on specific chakras requires many years' training. At the beginning think only of balancing these energy centres.

CHAPTER 10

Distant Healing

The Tao person abides in peace:
Reaching out
In a community of heart.
Regarding all that exists
As one family.

(TAO 49)

The Importance of Distant Healing

Distant healing is a very important aspect of a healer's repertoire. It is an application that healers working on their own or novice healers can use extensively. We have already seen that time and space are no barrier to the effectiveness of this approach. The healing will be every bit as successful as if the person were present in the room.

Distant healing also has the advantage that it can be directed not only to individuals but also to situations. At a global level there are many things happening on the planet today that could benefit from this form of balancing energy. The more that this is directed to areas of turmoil the less traumatic will be their resolution.

Healing in Work Situations

Individually it can also be used in work situations, where you have to interact with others. Other people's energies can have an important impact on our lives. Working in a school, hospital or a business puts us into situations where the disturbed thoughts of some individuals can easily upset our equilibrium and also the harmony of the group. Sending balancing healing thoughts can have enormous beneficial rewards. As has been said your outer life is a reflection of what is taking place within. If you are in a working environment of any description, it is an aspect of yourself. All working environments involving people will bring up tensions from time to time. As a healer, in a disagreeable workplace, you can bring positive Ch'i to bear to harmonise any difficulties that abound. This can be a great challenge, for sometimes we are seemingly forced into working for companies and organisations that cause us a great deal of inner stress.

When you come to give healing to these situations there are two approaches that can be adopted. One is to apply the self-healing techniques given in Chapter 5, where you consciously bring the people into your inner life to balance them. Alternatively you can send healing thoughts directly into the workplace in a general sense. In this way by healing your outer world you are also healing an inner part of you. A simple exercise to achieve this is given next.

EXERCISE

Healing Your Working Environment

(five minutes)

Aim: *To help colleagues find a good working relationship.*

- Adopt your normal meditation position and go through all your normal procedures for sending healing.cross within the circle), the lotus and the caduceus.

- Think of a central location within your office or place of work and project into the centre of it a symbol of harmony and balance.*
- Imagine the energy from this symbol exuding out to fill the whole of the space and the individuals contained within it.
- When you have completed this bring yourself back to full waking consciousness.

*There are many different symbols that you could use from the list given in Chapter 4. Some good general ones include the Celtic cross (equidistant cross within the circle), the lotus and the caduceus.

You can do this exercise from the sanctuary of your own home. When you are in the place of work reinforce the symbol from time to time by sending it a thought. You will also need to monitor how the people in your environment respond to the symbol. They will all pick it up at an unconscious level and some might find it difficult. If so, modify the symbol. Also, in some cases the chaotic elements that exist within some individuals may try to nullify its effects. This can sometimes happen in classroom situations. In these cases you will need to keep reinforcing the energy until you are successful.

Distant Healing in Groups

Distant healing also lends itself to being directed within the context of a group. Group healing provides the opportunity for a considerable stepping up of power. This is why many individuals find meditating within a group so much more effective than doing it on their own. The group dynamic gives a boost to the energy that can take everyone to a much deeper level.

The key to successful group healing is harmony and this cannot be stressed enough. Within every group a period of time should be spent, in each session that you come together, in working on harmonising and blending your energies. The success of your healing will be in direct proportion to your ability to achieve this.

If two healers come together and can harmonise their energies, the power of the healing is increased many fold. Put another way if each healer on their own can channel 2 litres of healing energy, combining their force will make 8 litres available to them. Each person added will similarly step up this energy, but only on the proviso that harmony is generated. If disharmony or tension occurs then the effectiveness of the group will be greatly reduced.

EXERCISE

Group Harmonising

(five minutes)

Aim: *To balance the energies of a group.*

- Try, wherever possible, to sit in a circle (this represents spirit). Ideally all members of the group should be on the same level either sitting on chairs or cushions on the floor. I realise that this is not always possible but it is an ideal. Someone should also lead the group to set the timing.
- Carry out the **body awareness exercise** and connect with your inner light.
- Imagine a feeling of harmony and love flowing from this light around the circle, either in a clockwise direction or both ways at once.

- Try and see this feeling as a coloured light. Then slowly sense that you are blending your colour with the colours that are travelling around so that you create between you a ribbon of light.
- Now try and imagine that you are blending your light with the other colours so that eventually they merge together to become white light.
- Hold this energy for a short period before bringing yourselves back to full conscious awareness.

You can carry out this exercise with one other person just as easily as with a group. It is also a very interesting exercise to carry this out with aspects of nature, particularly trees. Next time you are in a wood or near some trees, try to connect to them in this way.

Creating harmony in a group is challenging for it means accepting fully individuals for whom and what they are. It also means being clear and up front about your feelings. Every member of a group is important and has something valuable to contribute. We can all learn from the humblest of comments or insights. Sometimes individuals join groups and will express concepts that the other members do not wish to hear. Because of the law of polarities, we will attract to us those who can provide balance for the group. Always look at what is being said and try to integrate the comments within your psyche. If you spend time working on creating the harmony, those who are not meant to be in the group will leave of their own accord.

This can be a difficult concept to appreciate. But like those emotions that we find difficult and will often reject within ourselves, when we reject a member of a group, it is a reflection of an inner rejection. Splitting this part off by expelling the person will always ultimately backfire. This does not mean that one difficult individual should dominate the whole group. If you do not agree with what is being proposed you need to be clear in your own truth and speak it freely.

Healing Individuals

The simplest way when sending healing to a single individual is to imagine them sitting in front of you. Then in your mind send healing to them in exactly the same way as if they were present. When you have completed this, offer them up into an imagined light. Another way is to send the healing to wherever they are residing, sensing that the energy is balancing them in whatever way is most appropriate. Within group healing, the easiest way is to create a healing light in the centre of the circle and place in this light the person who needs help. Some groups will read out the names of the people who are to be sent healing. It is better when carrying out this form of healing not to hold each individual in the light for too long a period. Half a minute would normally be ample.

One problem that often crops up with distant healing groups is how long to continue sending the healing. If the group meets weekly I would recommend that healing be sent for no more than three months, unless there is a specific request to continue.

Healing World Situations

There are many situations within the world that need a great deal of healing, either by individuals working on their own or through a group. This can be done in the form of prayer by directing Ch'i healing to situations. The strongest and most powerful method is to focus the Ch'i as a 'love' energy and project this to the situation in general. This energy carries protection at its highest and will stop any chaotic energy coming back to you from the situation. The exercise given below is one that I use regularly within groups but it can equally well be carried out on your own. You should know that any help you give to the planet in this way will be used to the greatest benefit of all. Your reward will be knowing you are doing something very positive to help the transitions that are taking place.

EXERCISE

World Healing

(five to ten minutes)

***Aim:** To sending healing Ch'i to help balance world situations.*

- Carry out the **body awareness exercise** and connect to your inner light.
- If working with others link your energy together by imagining a golden circle of light surrounding the group.
- Draw upon your healing Ch'i and project this lovingly into the centre of the circle, so that an imaginary ball of light is created.
- Place a scaled-down version of planet earth into the centre of this light. You can imagine it in exactly the same way that an astronaut would see the earth from outer space.

- Send your healing on to the planet, focusing on any areas that need special attention. Try also to be aware of the other kingdoms, like the trees and animals.
- Finish by offering up the earth into the light above and see all your remaining Ch'i flowing out to the planet.
- Disconnect and close down in the same way that you would in an ordinary healing exercise.

All the above exercises can be carried out either on your own, with a friend or in a group. It does not really matter. All expression of Ch'i in a yang way will benefit both you and the person to whom it is being directed. Remember always to offer this healing to the highest aspect of the individual or situation that you are working upon. Also, when carrying out any healing with another person spend time connecting and harmonising your energies together. The rewards will be tremendous.

Summary

- Distant healing works as effectively as healing with the patient present.
- It can be applied either in groups or individually to a person or any type of situation.
- Within a group context the success of the healing will depend upon the harmony generated within the group.
- Groups can generate greater levels of energy than an individual on their own.

CHAPTER 11

Specialist Healing

When people regard one thing as beautiful
Something else is ugly.
By calling one thing good,
Its opposite becomes evil.
Yet having and not having balance each other.

(TAO 2)

There are some types of conditions that require specialist attention. In one sense every case is unique, and all have their variations from whatever we regard as the norm. However, certain cases need to be dealt with in a very specific way in order to ensure maximum benefit to both patient and healer. This chapter will focus on the following types of cases:

- ancestral healing;
- karmic healing;
- mental illness;
- psychic disturbances;
- cancer cases.

Ancestral Healing

The Importance of Ancestors

This is one of the most fascinating branches of healing that at present gets very little attention. As already indicated, a proportion of all our patterns stem from our genetic pool. In many cultures, both sophisticated and primitive, a great deal of attention is given to the ancestral family, for ancestor worship is one of the most widespread of all religious belief systems. In Taoism, time is regularly set aside for consulting the ancestors and prayers are offered up on their behalf. The ancestors were seen as having a direct link with the spiritual world and therefore in a position to bring positive benefit to the family. It was perhaps also intuitively realised how directly their energies affected the world of the living relatives. At a spiritual level time and space impose no restrictions so, in one sense, your ancestors are living concurrently with you. This can be a hard concept to take on board because the Western mind has become conditioned into thinking only in linear terms. Other cultures, not so restricted, accepted a much greater fluidity in the movement between the past, present and the future. Their ancestors were alive and connected to them. In propitiating the departed, the living were positively helping the flow of Ch'i in their lives.

In Western culture we have forgotten much of this inner knowing, for how many of us regularly think about or even remember our grandparents, let alone our great grandparents? From my own experience it is generally not necessary to go back further than your great grandparents' generation, although the Bible talks about the sins of the fathers 'even unto the third and *fourth* generation' that is to say your great great grandparents.

Ancestral Patterns

The concept behind this form of healing is quite simple. It suggests that where traumas, problems or strong types of behaviour have occurred with one or other of your forebears, the energy from this experience gets passed on to future generations. This is so even if the experience happens after the direct offspring have been born. Conversely, if you heal one of the ancestral patterns it becomes immediately available to your own offspring. The reason why this should happen is I believe based on 'resonance'. We carry at a genetic level the resonant patterns of our forebears which, like a radio set tuned to our ancestors, allows a transfer of energy or information to take place. Healing this type of situation can be carried out in exactly the same way that you would apply 'distant' healing. You do not need to have a clear picture in your mind of the way that an ancestor looked for the healing to be effective.

In his book *Healing the Family Tree*, Dr Kenneth McAll recounts a case of a woman in her early thirties who suddenly developed a fear of water. Researching into her family patterns she found that an uncle had died in the Titanic disaster. A healing service was carried out in which the uncle was 'committed . . . to the Lord'. Healing this ancestor freed the woman from her phobia. In most cases it is only necessary to deal with your direct ancestors, that is your parents, grandparents and great grandparents, but in some cases, such as the one just cited, healing another relative may also be appropriate.

It is an interesting supposition that the enmity felt between the Arabs and the Jews could have an ancestral cause. Both trace their origins back to Abraham; the Arabs tracing their descent through Ishmael the eldest, but illegitimate son, while the Jews are descended from Isaac. Had both sons been treated evenly, perhaps the present level of antagonism between these two races might not have occurred. In a similar way there are a number of aristocratic families in Britain who have family 'curses' that appear to run inexorably down through the generations. Healing such situations must be based upon forgiveness and the acknowledgement of each other's rights.

Before you can consider helping others in healing ancestral patterns this way you first need to work on your own forebears. Sometimes the traumas carried by our ancestors can be very powerful and in these cases it can be beneficial to work with a therapist or friend. I have worked with a number of people on ancestral healing with some amazing insights and release of blocked energy.

Ancestral Myths

Ancestral myths, too numerous to mention here, abound in many cultures. We saw in the story of Isis and Osiris that Osiris was cut into 14 pieces. This is a curious number that does not find echo in other traditions. However, it is worth noting that 14 is the sum total of your ancestors back to your great grandparents' gener-

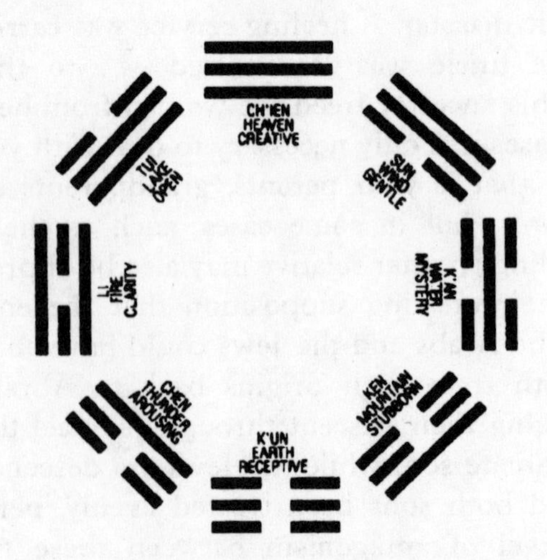

The eight tri-grams of the I Ching (Pa Kua)

ation. Adding your parents (2), to your grandparents (4) and your great grandparents (8) gives 14 ancestors in all. It could well be that part of the symbolism of this myth is to do with healing our genetic patterning, through our forebears. In the myth Osiris is reconstructed by Isis which relates to the 'love' principle within.

Also your family tree chart mirrors exactly the developing tri-grams of the I Ching of Ancient China. This starts off with two lines yang (—) and yin (— —) and progresses in 2 stages to the 8 tri-grams that are the basis of the 64 hexagrams. While I have never come across any direct reference to this symbolic link, I cannot believe that it is a coincidence bearing in mind the enormous emphasis on the ancestors in Chinese culture.

Ancestral Chart

To start the process of ancestral healing you will need to construct a chart along the lines of the one set out here and fill in as much detail as you can. It does not matter if there are blanks. Next, consider whether any problems you are experiencing in your present life were similarly found in other known members of the family. If so, the cause almost certainly lies within the family tree. If you do not know upon which side to look you can either use a pendulum to dowse for the answer, or, alternatively, I often get students to imagine that a bright coloured spotlight is shining on their chart indicating which ancestor needs to be worked on. It is fascinating how often the obvious is not highlighted, but the attention is drawn to another of the forebears. Another method is to make up a set of 14 cards marking on each a separate ancestor. These can then be shuffled and an ancestor selected. Once this is done carry out the following exercise.

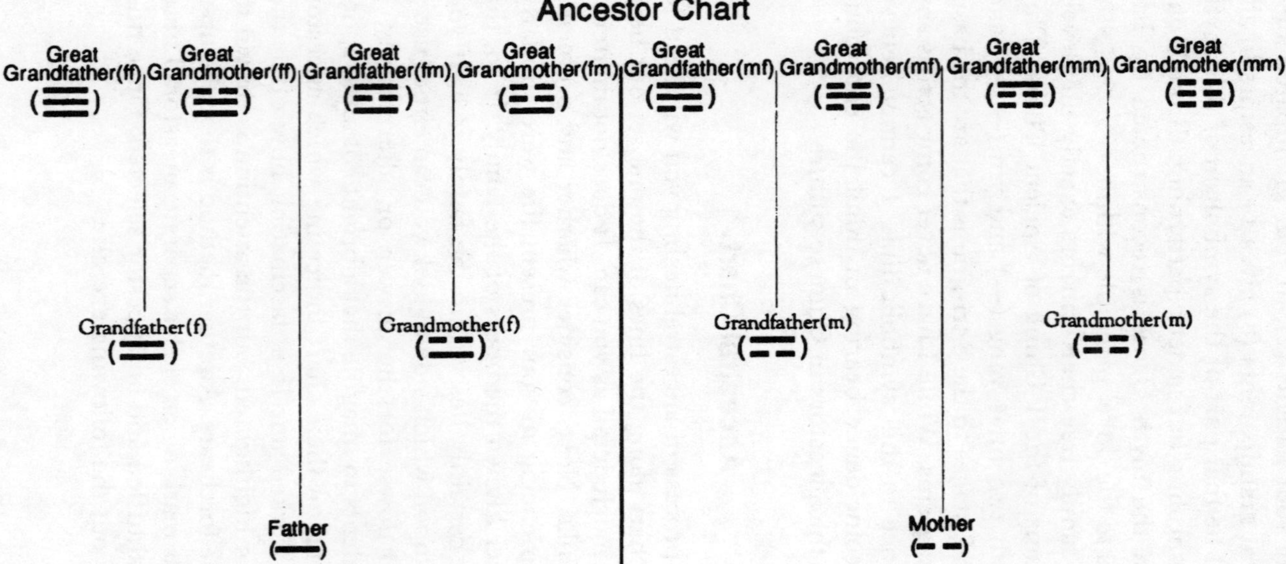

Set up a chart on a large piece of paper, similar to the above, and fill in as much detail as you can, including dates of birth and death, illnesses, number of children and any special information that you know. Leave blanks if no information is known.

Note: Associated I Ching lines in brackets. ▬▬ = yang line ▬ ▬ = yin line (f) = father's side (m) = mother's side

EXERCISE

Ancestral Healing

(ten to fifteen minutes)

Aim: *To clear and heal blocked energy within your family tree.*

- Adopt your normal meditation posture, carry out the **body awareness exercise** and connect to your inner light.
- If you have not already done so, look at the chart and imagine that a 'golden light' is shining on the ancestor who most needs integrating and balancing as an energy within you.
- 'Tune into' that ancestor, and try and sense what it is that needs healing and then carry out the normal healing procedure given in Chapter 5.
- When you have completed this part of the exercise, sense or imagine that the new healing pattern is flowing down from that ancestor to yourself.
- See this energy integrated within your own being.
- Send a thought of thanks and acknowledgement to the ancestor before carrying out the closing down exercise.

Note: In some particular situations the most powerful energy for helping these types of cases has been found to be that of the 'Christ spirit'. It may be this is appropriate because it is a quality that the ancestor normally would have been most familiar with. Alternatively, it may be because so much healing at this level requires forgiveness that 'Christ' energy is the most relevant.

This type of healing can be applied to all sorts of conditions stemming from your ancestral tree. For example, if you are suffering from arthritis and there is a predisposition to arthritis in your family, you can move back to an earlier ancestor who expressed this complaint. Carry out the healing in exactly the same way that you would with distant healing on a real person. You might need to do this on a number of occasions, seeking also to balance this on an emotional and mental level, as well as the physical. Finally, when you have completed the healing, sense that it is coming through the family tree to yourself. This exercise can be repeated until you have got to know and balance the energies of all your main ancestors. They will then become an integrated aspect of yourself and freed of any blocks that they might be carrying. On the other side of the coin, as soon as you free blocks within yourself at this level it immediately releases this dynamic for your children, if you have any, so in a way you are also healing future generations.

Healing Others

If I am giving healing to a person and sense that there is some pattern from the family tree that is impacting on their life, I will carry out a standard healing treatment on the ancestor and then look to integrate this within the individual. For example, if I sensed that a trauma from a grandparent was affecting the life of a client, then I would spend time giving healing directly to that ancestor, before finally sensing that energy being re-integrated within the person.

Further Study

Those interested in further exploration and study into the healing of ancestral and family patterns should read my book *Healing Your Family Patterns* (Piatkus) 1997, which contains more information and exercises.

Karmic Healing

Karmic Patterns

In the sense that karma is an expression of law of 'cause and effect', then all dis-ease is karmic. However, this term is usually applied to those cases where the cause appears to stem from a previous life or lives. At one level it is not necessary to go back into a past life to sort out a problem that has manifested within this life-span. There will always be opportunities for resolving the dis-ease, in whatever way it presents itself, within the context of this present life. Yet for some, connecting back and resolving a past life trauma can produce very dramatic changes. It is one of those branches of healing that can be amazingly effective if you have a belief structure and openness to exploring healing from the standpoint of a past incarnation. Equally, if you cannot accept the concept of reincarnation, you should not feel that this will prevent the healing process. In my experience past life traumas will generally show up initially within childhood and they can be resolved at this level if you wish.

Discerning Karmic Patterns

The simplest way to discern karmic patterns is to look at the patterns that operate through your present life. To do this properly you will need to write down on a sheet of paper the key elements of your life as follows:

- fears;
- habits;
- belief structures;
- relationships which are both enhancing and difficult;
- types and periods of physical illness.

Any deep seated or repeating patterns from the above list will often have a past-life constituent and can be tackled through karmic healing or past-life therapy.

Sometimes individuals, either through dreams or from a spontaneous regression, will remember a part of a previous existence that gave birth to an underlying problem. In this cases there is an easy entry point, in the recovered memory, to resolving the pattern.

Healing Karmic Patterns

Personally, where possible, I have adopted the procedure outlined in Chapter 2. That is, I have visited the place or places associated with the underlying problem that needs shifting and while there, carried out a meditation incorporating a healing or forgiveness exercise. I will always try to understand the reasons for the underlying pattern, for this speeds up the healing process. In my experience it is not necessary to relive the trauma to release it, but you will need to acknowledge and accept its relevance. For example, if you believed that you had been burnt at the stake, you do need to fully re-experience and act out all the emotions that lay behind this traumatic happening. What you will need to do is acknowledge those emotions and see them as part of you in order for healing to take place.

In many cases, it is not possible or practical to visit a place in person, but you can always go there in your mind. If you felt, for example, that you wished to connect to a life in the Inca period in Peru, you can imagine yourself back in that epoch and allow whatever experiences that need to surface to come to the fore. If you trust the wisdom of your 'higher mind' it will bring forward what you need. Alternatively just feeling into the experience, without reference to a place or time, may be all that is necessary.

Healing Others

This type of healing can best be carried out effectively with the conscious co-operation of the individual. It is closely allied to past-life therapy, but involves a more energetic interaction in the healing process. The key elements can stem from an insight of the healer or from the patient who is aware of some past life pattern that is bothering them.

Ideally both healer and patient need to connect with that life and then work on healing the situation as it manifested then. Let us suppose that an individual died of starvation as a child in a previous life. In this life they find they have a craving for food that is so compulsive that they have become overweight. (As a tip, whenever any extreme symptom is presented always look for the answer in the opposite.) The healer can first help the person connect back to the source of the problem, in this case the starving child. By sending healing to that part to balance its energy, and then seeing it integrate within the present life, a form of re-balance can be achieved. The child within can start to recognise that it is no longer starving. Powerful experiences get carried forward on the basis of the original imbalance and by awakening the child to its true reality the compulsive energy is dissipated. As healers we need then to help the person in the present life consciously integrate these energies.

This method can be used for all sorts of conditions, but we should remember that only a small proportion of cases need to be treated in this way. To be tidy also, we can look upon past lives as a series of filing cabinets. When we access into a past life it is like opening up one of the drawers. When we have finished that drawer should be closed again, and a sense of integration be sent within the whole. If we go on opening lots of drawers without closing them, it can have exactly the same effect as in a real filing cabinet. It will fall over. There are very good reasons, as already mentioned, why we do not normally remember our previous existences.

Mental Illness and Psychic Disturbances

These types of cases fall broadly into the category of psychiatric disorders and psychic dysfunction. They include spirit possession, schizophrenia, drug and alcohol addiction, psychic disturbances (i.e. poltergeist phenomena) and 'curses'. They are some of the most tricky situations to diagnose accurately and often hardest to correct. **They require specialist help from the medical profession and should never be tackled by healers in isolation or without specialist training.** This is a very broad subject and one that can but be touched upon in this work. But as healers we are likely to meet such cases from time to time and shared information can be helpful. In this section I have also included details on healing cancer cases of all types as there are some similarities with the above.

The border between sanity and mental illness is often very thin. This is perhaps why in the past, in Western society at least, such fear surrounded all forms of psychic development. The individual who hears 'voices' might either be a St Joan or a psychiatric patient. What separates the two is probably only how they have managed to integrate this aspect into their lives, and who is prepared to believe them. Many individuals have no doubt 'been committed' in the past because they have made such claims.

There can be many underlying reasons why a breakdown occurs between the spiritual self or soul and other aspects of the personality. Before considering the 'spiritual' or 'psychic' perspective on the above we need first to understand how the medical profession views such cases.

The Medical Perspective

It is normal to classify mental illness into a number of main groups. These include:

- neuroses;
- psychoses;
- organic mental disorders;
- psychoactive substance use disorders;
- disorders of infancy, childhood and adolescence;
- mental retardation.

Neurosis

In neurotic illness there is an exaggeration of one aspect of the personality or behavioural pattern that becomes incapacitating. Phobias and obsessions fall into this category. The individual realises that something is wrong but is not necessarily able to control their problem. Their personality and intellectual ability remains intact, although their lives are impaired to a greater or lesser degree according to the severity of the condition.

Psychosis

Psychotic conditions involve the whole personality which becomes seriously dysfunctional, affecting emotional and mental states. Their abnormal behaviour, emotional swings, and bizarre, exaggerated beliefs easily alienate the sufferer from other members of society. Psychotic illness also falls into two groups:

- manic-depressive psychosis;
- schizophrenia.

In manic-depressive psychosis there are extreme mood swings between high elation and deep depression. In some cases the individual becomes stuck in either the elation or depression. In its milder form, it is also strangely linked with great creativity. Many famous artists and comedians have suffered elements of this illness.

Schizophrenia is a widespread illness affecting about one per cent of the population. It is found in all societies including primitive cultures. The word 'schizophrenia' means 'split mind' and was first coined by German psychiatrist Eugen Bleuler in 1911. Its symptoms can be classified as:

- disorders of thinking;
- disorders of feeling;
- delusions;
- hallucinations;
- disturbances of movement.

It often arises in the late teens but can occur at any time in life. It can last for short periods where a specific stress has brought it on, such as pregnancy, or it can be long term.

Organic mental disorders

These illnesses have an organic constituent in the deterioration of the brain or nerve cells such as in dementia, Alzheimer's disease, Parkinson's disease and alcohol poisoning.

Psychoactive substance use disorders

These include intoxication, dependence and withdrawal of alcohol and addictive drugs such as cocaine and hallucinogens. (It should be appreciated that many foods or substances taken into the body can have a damaging effect upon subtle balance between the soul and the physical. Allergic reactions to some substances can give rise to mental illness and these should be checked for in any treatment.)

Disorders of infancy, childhood and adolescence

Into this category come dyslexia, autism and hyperkinetic disorder.

Mental retardation

These disorders can range from mild to severe and include genetic based abnormalities such as Down's syndrome.

Spiritual Overview

From a 'spiritual' perspective mental illness and psychic disturbance can arise from a number of causes. Often such cases fall into more than one category but broadly speaking they can be grouped as follows:

Soul level conditions

This can take three forms:

- Where the spiritual self is not able to cope with an aspect or aspects of physical incarnation. This can be because it is a 'young' soul or because of a past-life memory. When this happens a rift occurs between the spiritual self and the 'ego' mind. All sorts of events can trigger this off including the death of a partner, loss of job, unsatisfactory marriage and so on. As well as psychotic conditions, a whole host of minor conditions, including mental breakdowns, depression and dementia, can be classed under this heading. Sometimes these events can cause part of the psyche or sub-personalities to split off and assume an independent reality within the individual. This can sometimes seem like a 'possession' case but is in fact part of the individual's own psyche at odds within itself.
- Where the inner core essence of the soul is shattered

from a deep inner trauma. When this form of imbalance manifests in early childhood, a past life cause must be suspected.

- Where, for whatever reason, the spiritual self has chosen to undergo the experience of mental illness or defect. In these cases the core essence is not in itself damaged. Down's syndrome cases can often be an example of this.

Invasions

This is where an outside or alien destructive energy, generally in the form of a spirit being, has invaded the psychic space disrupting the normal flow of communication between the spiritual self and the mind. Cases where you might find this include multiple personality, possession, drug and alcohol addiction, hallucinations, 'hearing voices', 'curses' and schizophrenia. These invasions are sometimes referred to as 'dopplegangers'. Invasive energies can also come down through the family tree as indicated in the section on ancestral healing.

Psychic Problems

Covers all aspects where imbalances occur in the psychic activity of an individual. 'Healing voices', poltergeist phenomena, and over-sensitivity to atmospheres can be included here.

Healing Treatment

The following information is included for experienced healers who are already working within a group context. On no account should these cases be tackled by novice healers.

Invasions

These can be some of the most tricky cases to deal with from the healer's stance. Invasions occur when an outside energy or spirit being attaches itself to an individual, with the intention of negatively influencing the 'host's' life to suit itself. All of us at different times are assisted by spiritual presences from the non-physical realms. The intention of these beings is to help us unfold the life pattern that we have chosen in this particular life. So being influenced is a natural part of physical incarnation. In these cases the intention of that spiritual presence is directed to helping us fulfil our lives.

Where invasion occurs this intention becomes distorted, and the influencing spirit no longer has our best interests at heart, but is only thinking of itself. An example of this is with drug addiction.

Drug addictions

When a drug addict dies, his or her soul is faced by a terrible dilemma. For whatever period in their life that the addiction lasted, a form of powerful experience had been achieved by the use of a chemical substance put into the body. Because 'resonance', that which we experience within the spiritual self, affects the body and that which we experience within the body affects the spiritual self, drugs then become a form of 'spiritual experience'. However, after death the addict suddenly finds that by not having a physical body, he or she is no longer able to gain this form of 'spiritual high'. Now at first glance this may seem a good thing, as the addict will be forced into a metaphorical 'drying out house'. But as all those who treat addicts know, in order to provide a cure, the addict must first wish to change. Without that desire the situation is hopeless. Exactly the same type of experience occurs on a spiritual level. The dis-embodied soul of the addict, then in a state of considerable distress, experiencing a form of spiritual 'cold turkey' and rejecting spiritual help, will be drawn back inexorably to those individuals and places that it knew whilst in incarnation. It will then attempt to latch itself on to some other unfortunate addict to gain a form of secondary experience through that person. So a type of 'possession' takes place. The therapist or psychiatrist trying to help has therefore to contend not only with the individual but also with this other subtle invasion, that naturally does everything in its power to discourage an abstention from drugs. A very similar situation occurs with alcoholics and a downward self-perpetuating spiral ensues.

Invasions of a person's psychic space have many degrees to them, from an insidious nudging to a full-blown take over. Sometimes individuals through a past life experience can become totally dominated by another spirit. Others can become 'possessed' through a deliberate misuse of psychic energy for malefic purposes; like the story of Dr Faustus. Many criminal acts have been encouraged by subtle influences from departed souls.

Destructive spirit influences

Unfortunately because a person dies, it does not automatically mean that their soul becomes all wise; far from it. Some souls become enmeshed in a spiral of chaotic and destructive energies particularly if they have been subjected to these influences in their life. Such souls will often reject all higher level help that is offered to them and seek revenge on society by encouraging all forms of antisocial and destructive behaviour. This is why it is very important to help the criminal element. Certainly some individuals need to be restrained in detention centres or prison, but they also need to be helped. Should they die with feelings of anger, hatred and resentment against society, that is far from the end of their story. They can continue to exact revenge from beyond the grave by a persistent damaging influence on the minds and psyches of others. Eventually, if we accept the concept of reincarnation, they could come back again into a physical body only to continue the destructive whirlpool from the previous life.

All individuals who have antisocial tendencies need help and they should be treated in ways that will allow them to change their patterns of behaviour. As history has shown, even the most hardened criminal, with the right assistance, can make remarkable recoveries and go on to make a positive contribution to society.

Removing invading spirits

It does not really matter what the cause of invasion is, if this is suspected. The first step has to be to remove the invading spirit. This is where potential problems can arise for like the 'dog in the manger', they are not generally going to go quietly. The main difficulty is that, under cosmic law, if two forces meet the stronger will always come out on top. It does not matter what your intentions are. If in the physical world you try to stop a bully beating a child, then he or she could just as easily turn on you. If he or she is the stronger, then you will suffer the consequences and get beaten up yourself. Unfortunately it happens all too regularly nowadays. This is why when tackling such cases, you need to work with others. After all, two people would stand a better chance with our bully, than one. Even then extreme caution should be employed.

My own preference is always to carry out such clearings or 'exorcisms' from a distance. I respect the intentions of those who will try and work directly with an individual, but I sometimes feel this gets in the way of the clearing activity. In cases where the native spirit is trying to resist the invasion it is not quite so difficult to remove the interloper. There is a willing co-operation from the patient. Cases of dominance are much harder because the person has become conditioned to feel subservient. If the spirit is removed completely it will often be drawn back by the person concerned. In the latter cases, the 'exorcism' needs to be a very gradual process. In these situations it is often better to start by just sending healing to both the possessing entity and native soul so that they can begin to let go of their reliance upon each other.

In all cases the invading spirit needs a great deal of help and healing. They should be treated firmly but kindly and every effort made to help them adjust their perspective.

Possession or not?

There are many types of cases that can seem like possession but are not. Because two or more distinct personalities present themselves, do not automatically assume that they are being possessed or invaded. Aspects within someone's own psyche will often vie for dominance of the mind.

This is also a very emotive area and brings up all sorts of fears within individuals, made no better by some of the lurid films that we see. Such examples grossly distort what actually takes place. Exorcism need be no more dramatic than any other healing case.

To tackle this type of condition you need to have a good diagnostic insight into what is going on. In my work with a psychiatric doctor, dealing with mental illness cases from hospital, it is fascinating how perceptive a psychic diagnosis can sometimes be using just the name of the individual. The major difference between the allopathic diagnosis and the psychic diagnosis is the insight into the underlying cause of the problem, which rarely lies on just a physical level.

A number of years ago, I had met up with a woman who came originally from Canada. She had left her country because of an entanglement with a psychic group, which she had started to have serious reservations about. She had been staying at our house for a few days and in passing conversation wondered if she might be pregnant. 'Tuning in' I was immediately aware of a spirit standing alongside, and assumed that it must be the baby. She seemed accepting of this, but naturally wished to get this medically confirmed. The tests came back negative; I was perplexed.

'Tuning in' again, I could still see this spirit standing on her left. Something made me feel uneasy, although on the surface it appeared to be fine. So I carried out an exercise that in esoteric circles is called the Law of Challenge. I demanded that the spirit in question reveal its true identity. The mask fell away and what resided underneath was far from pleasant. I then had to quickly clear the spirit off and rebalance the energy of the woman. She immediately felt relief and the next day her periods started up again. This spirit had clearly attached itself to her while in the group and was subtly influencing her actions.

Let me again emphasise that in carrying out this clearing there was no writhing on the ground or foaming at the mouth. Indeed, in all my years of healing I have only once witnessed that type of response and for very different reasons. Healing these situations can be like any other. It can, of course, be dressed up with all sorts of ritualistic practices, but this is not necessary.

Another case involved a woman who claimed that she was being possessed by a man. 'Tuning in' to her I could not see any spirit entity, so I asked her to describe what she saw. The figure was of a large powerful man, dressed in black, standing over her with a knife, trying to murder her. She kept emphasising, 'He is trying to murder me'. A flash of insight prompted me to challenge her, 'Who is it you are trying to murder?' The release of energy was both dramatic and cathartic. All her pent-up anger and split-off hatred came pouring out. Her murderous intent was directed in this instant towards her husband with feelings which, up to that point, had been too terrible for her to own. This was the start of a full release from this problem, which took a few more months to complete. This case is an example of a split within the psyche. Interestingly the obvious solution in both these cases was not the correct one.

Soul Level Conditions

In their most extreme expressions these are some of the hardest cases to help. Perhaps, more accurately, their treatment should be seen as much more long term. There are rarely quick results. What can show dramatic improvement are phobias and obsessions that stem from a previous life or ancestral patterns. If the underlying cause can be discovered and the trauma re-integrated within the psyche then dramatic changes can occur. My own example of biting my finger nails is a mild form of this type of situation. Both Dr Roger Woolger in his book *Other Lives, Other Selves* and Dr Denis Kelsey in his book *Many Lifetimes*, give good examples of this type of recovery.

Soul choices

Some souls choose to be born into a body with mental defects. In these cases we have to respect the wishes of the spiritual self for the experiences that it has chosen to undergo. Healing will help the person gain the greatest benefit from these experiences and can enormously improve the quality of that life. I have known a number of such cases where, paradoxically, one of the main reasons for the incarnation was to provide an experience for the parents or family. Spirits or souls will often work together over a number of lives, incarnating into similar families and providing a complementary experience for each other. The mentally handicapped child will challenge the parents to face the unacceptable side of their own nature. If they can meet that challenge by caring for, and bringing up their offspring, an enormous karmic release takes place. Because of the interconnectedness that occurs at a resonant level such children are a barometer for what is happening within the dynamic of the other members of the family. The challenge of every parent is to face up to the corresponding part of themselves that the child expresses. Healing in these cases should also be sent to the whole family.

Young souls

This concept can only be satisfactorily understood in terms of reincarnation. It is based on the notion that new or young souls, without previous physical experience, are incarnating all the time. If the 'new soul' is born into a family and life pattern that is balanced and protected then, like a new baby, it has every chance of growing to maturity in a healthy way. Unfortunately much of human life can be traumatic and this can present the 'young soul' with many problems. The easiest way for any soul to deal with a difficult situation is to retreat from it. This occurs when at a soul level the individual is not able to integrate or come to terms with the physical, emotional or psychological experience that is confronting them. An example of this is where a person's pressurised job is at odds with their psychological make-up and ability to cope. This can eventually lead to mental illness or breakdown where the soul starts to detach itself from the body, causing a split in the psyche. In this latter example the pressures of modern living and our mental beliefs can cause problems for 'older' souls, so a mental breakdown in itself should not be seen as evidence for a 'young' soul.

Entering into physical incarnation for some souls is rather like testing the water of a hot bath. The spiritual self, during childhood and adolescence, gradually links itself down into the body, but can, when faced with difficult situations (the bath is too hot), immediately retreat within itself. This causes a rift within the psychic structure of the individual and upsets the rhythm of life. Schizophrenia in adolescence is an extreme aspect of this condition. If the outer world situation is corrected then very often everything can be brought back to a state of balance.

In later life similar types of situation can occur leading to dementia or other psychiatric conditions, before the soul finally separates itself completely from the body at death. Where the soul or mind is not able to accept or integrate any situation then part of the psyche can become split off, and appear to have a level of reality on its own. The healing case mentioned on page 237 is an aspect of this type of condition. Fortunately in this particular case the individual was able to re-own the murderous part of her that she had disowned.

Healing treatments

Helping all these types of conditions needs to take place on a number of fronts. At one level, drugs can play an important part in providing a form of physical and mental relief. They will at least sedate the effects of the imbalance on the body. Ideally they should only be seen as a short term solution, for the real cause of imbalance lies on other levels. Many different forms of complementary therapy such as reflexology, aromatherapy and naturopathy can be beneficial. Healing is always appropriate and needs to be sent to the spiritual self and in particular to its linkage with the mind. In mental illness cases I will also work directly on the sub-personality aspects, trying to help them re-integrate themselves. Counselling or psychotherapy, where practical, should also be given to assist the person in balancing and acknowledging the various aspects of their personality. Clearly there are some cases that will require lifelong medication. However, the more that this form of healing can be brought to bear, the greater will be the benefits and improvements to those in need.

Plumbing the depths

Within our society we tend to fight shy of plumbing the depths of who and what we are. When extreme situations of depression arise,the first tendency is to try and get out of that state as quickly as possible, like an individual in a swamp. Actually if we could allow ourselves the opportunity to really feel into it, explore it, sit with it, then it would lessen of its own volition. Counselling and psychotherapy can play a very valuable role in these cases. I have also worked with many clients using visual imagery to shift levels of awareness and help balance the polarities that exist within.

Shattered souls

In the previous cases, the soul or spiritual self, in broad terms, is reasonably healthy in that it has a coherence about it. However, grave defects within the soul can sometimes come through causing a warp from a very deep level within the core essence of that individual. An example of this is where a soul re-incarnates again immediately after a traumatic death, without giving itself sufficient time to process the experience in the after-life. The chaotic experiences from the former life can impact so strongly upon the present that it is very difficult for the individual to find any sense of balance. There is not the space here to go into all the ways that these soul level aberrations can occur but needless to say that, in their extreme forms, such cases will show little improvement within the context of one life. Information on a particular case, illustrating this point, came through the channelled guidance of a 'spiritual teacher' many years ago. We had been sending healing to a particular individual, with a severe personality quirk, which we felt sure stemmed from a previous life. Checking on what more could be done, we were informed that his particular condition would take many lives to resolve, though the healing being offered was of benefit at a soul level.

Physical brain defects

In these cases there is an obvious cause for the mental imbalance. Where individuals, through accident or stroke, have suffered defects, much can often be done to help speed up recovery and repair some of the damage. Healing can be directed to the brain and etheric web of the head to help new connections to be made. The brain has an amazing capacity to repair damage or re-route information. There have been many cases where the prognosis has been very bad, with severe mental impairment suspected, and the individual has gone on to make a full recovery. There is always the potential for a complete healing if that is the wish of the spiritual self.

Strokes can sometimes be seen as another form of mental breakdown, where some aspect of the person's outer life is at complete odds with the inner world. The stoke is a dramatic way of pulling us up short and asking that we re-evaluate our lives. If this is done then the individual can often go on to lead a normal active life.

When brain defects occur during birth, or in early childhood, the solution can be a little more complex. In these cases the condition might well have arisen for one of the reasons given in the soul level causes mentioned previously. If so then a complete cure will be unlikely. Whatever the cause healing will help at a soul level.

At the other end of the life, dementia and similar illnesses often result when the soul is unable to accept some aspect of the life, perhaps the death of a loved one, and begins to retreat from the physical world. This opens up the possibility for the physical elements of a disease to take a hold of the body. The soul at this level is usually quite contented. It is the friends and relatives who often need the greatest help with healing in these cases.

Psychic Problems

Into this category come a whole host of conditions from over-sensitivity, to poltergeist phenomena. The latter includes many types of psychic disturbance. People will sometimes believe that their house is haunted because they hear strange noises and find objects have moved. Yet when one tunes in to this type of situation, instead of the house being haunted by a departed spirit, it is clear that the 'warped energy' is actually coming from one of the occupants. The classic poltergeist case will involve a child going through puberty. Energy from the sexual centre is released and often linked to aggressive feelings towards the parents that cannot be openly expressed. The resultant cocktail comes out as destructive energy causing physical phenomena within the house. To heal this situation you will need to balance the chakric centres of the child, and reset the energies of the house. Counselling may also have to be given, although generally with time the situation will subside of its own accord. Individuals with a lot of psychic power who do not properly express this energy can also attract other spirits to them. They will sometimes manipulate this force for their own ends. Healing here needs to be sent to the individual rather than just focusing on the house.

Another type of problem can occur around the dysfunction of electric appliances. Professor Jahn's experiments mentioned in Chapter 1 have shown how individuals can influence electrical circuits. When an individual has an excess of Ch'i energy that is not properly used it can sometimes 'earth' itself through light sockets or other electrical appliances. In the former case it will normally cause light bulbs to blow, in the latter it will cause appliances to break down. If this is happening to you, seek ways to use and balance your Ch'i energy through the methods mentioned in this book.

Hearing Voices

A number of causes can give rise to what is termed 'hearing voices'. It may be that the individual has a mediumistic ability and cannot recognise this. Such individuals will either need help developing this gift, or they will need assistance to close down these energies from within. This will mean working on their chakric centres as mentioned in the previous chapter. This type of problem can also arise from 'split' personality defects. In these cases, aspects of the person's own psyche begin to communicate as separate personality types. To heal these situations necessitates balancing and integrating the sub-personalities within. This condition often arises because the 'ego' is not able to accept a part of itself. Providing space in a therapeutic environment, to fully explore what is being said, can be a helpful part of the healing process.

Over-sensitivity can at one level be dealt with by encouraging the person to strengthen their protective auric shield. There could also be psychological reasons that will need to be addressed.

Cancer Cases

At an energetic level these cases are the result of a breakdown in the etheric/physical linkage. There can be many causes of this, including emotional traumas, physical injuries and toxic substances like tobacco being taken into the body. The energy behind cancer is very specific and this is why it requires specialist treatment from a healing perspective.

I realise that in presenting the following information I will not necessarily be conforming to the consensus view held by many healers and certainly not by orthodox medical practitioners. Knowledge on this subject first came to my attention from the same 'spiritual teacher' quoted previously. Experience has taught me its validity.

The energy behind a sarcoma is a form of alien invasion of the body. It stems from a particular spirit life form that is completely out of balance, and should not in fact be experiencing through the medium of the physical body at all. Another way of seeing this is as a form of large spiritual virus. Because of its imbalances, it is attracted to aspects within people that are also out of balance. It will normally enter our organism through one of the chakric centres and become embedded within the etheric web, before manifesting down on to a physical level.

Various forms of medical treatment can dislodge this invasion, such as chemotherapy, radiotherapy, and operations to remove the defective physical organ. Sometimes the patients themselves will rebalance those aspects within, and spontaneous remission occurs. There are many wonderful accounts to be found in the books of Richard Moss, Lawrence LeShan and Larry Dossey, exemplifying the road that can lead to recovery. Healers and therapists can help individuals awaken their inner potential. Every case of transformation demands radical change at some level. Even if it is just learning **to be**. However, at an energetic level we need to be very wary of not directly feeding the cancer with energy. Richard Moss calls cancer a 'high energy disease', if we put more energy into the cancer, the effect can be like putting a dose of fertiliser on to a plant.

Healing cancer treatment

The correct approach at an energetic level is to first and foremost balance the energies of the whole person. If the individual can throw off the cancer themselves this is the ideal. Secondly, the healer can attack the seat of the cancer by imagining that their healing Ch'i is shrinking the cancerous growth. This is the approach that some well-known healers adopt. Unless you feel confident about doing this, it is much better to focus just on the overall balance. The third option is to remove the 'cancer spirit' from the body, heal it and then offer it back to the cosmos for transformation. Again this should only be tackled by those who are experienced healers.

The ideal approach to helping those who have contracted this life threatening disease is to incorporate many of the methods offered by wholistic cancer centres such as the Bristol Cancer Centre in England. Diet, meditation, life reassessment, healing and orthodox medical treatment all have a part to play. We also need to accept the spiritual self's right to leave incarnation by whatever method it deems appropriate.

Healing terminal cases

Miracles do occur but we will all have to die at some time. Physical death is not the end, but a tiny moment in the continuum of who and what we are. Souls will often choose a terminal illness to leave incarnation. Sending strong healing or prayer to 'make the person well', or to keep them back, can be doing a grave disservice to the individual. This is why the healing must always be offered to the spiritual self for its choice on how it best wishes to be helped. If you sense that the soul wishes to move on then healing can be sent to assist that process. Healing should also be offered to other members of the family, for it is always they who suffer the most when a loved one leaves incarnation.

Summary

- Certain types of cases require specialist healing treatment. Such cases include mental and psychiatric problems as well as cancer.
- Ancestral healing works through balancing the

'Family Tree'.

- Karmic healing necessitates the re-balancing of energies from a past life.
- Accurate 'psychic' diagnosis is required to determine the underlying cause of the condition. We should not assume the obvious.
- Energy should not be directed to the location of cancer within a person.

CHAPTER 12

Balancing The Ch'i Of Places

Cultivated in your soul.
The Tao brings peace to your life.
Generated in your home,
It brings peace with those you love.
Spreading to friends and neighbours,
It brings peace to your community.

(TAO 54)

Balancing the Ch'i of places is an enormous subject. We can only touch the surface in this chapter. The field includes balancing the energies of your house and place of work, hauntings, earth energies, ley lines, geopathic stress, magnetic anomalies, underground streams, electromagnetic pollution and spiritual focal points from the Devic realm.

The Ch'i of Places

The energies of places are derived from a number of causes. Broadly speaking they can be divided into two main categories:

- those that have been generated by human beings;
- those that stem from the natural energies of the planet.

Into this second category we need to include both geophysical energies as well as the spiritual forces that hold the earth in balance. It lies within the range of human capability to be able to do a great deal to improve energies created by human beings, but you can only marginally affect the Ch'i of the planet.

Human beings interact with places through the type of activity that is carried on there. All thought and emotion leaves an imprint in the etheric web of a place. Because the etheric is close to the physical, these thoughts and emotions become locked into specific locations. Where work of a harmonious or spiritual nature is carried out, the resultant atmosphere is very pleasant and uplifting. Conversely, where murderous crimes and aggressive behaviour have occurred, the feeling in the atmosphere is very oppressive. This type of Ch'i is somewhat akin to radioactive energy, in that it only slowly decreases in its intensity. So events that happened a thousand years ago, while still present at an energetic level, do not have the same impact as events from, say the Second World War.

Most people are conscious of these differences in energy, although they do not often understand the reasons why they feel the way they do. Think of a place that you have visited recently. What did you feel about the place? Was it a comfortable feeling or one that left you cold? Fortunately, like refuse disposal, psychic or energetic rubbish that people have created can be cleaned up and recycled. At its simplest level, a room in a house can be cleared and the atmosphere reset in a few minutes. At the other end of the scale, some of the energies from the First and Second World Wars will take a considerable amount of time and effort to cleanse. Sad to relate we are still grossly polluting the planet to this day and the pollution that we see on a physical level is unfortunately reflected on many other levels.

Ch'i that has been generated within a place builds an atmosphere which will tend to attract to it similar types of expression. If a couple have been living in a house, holding a lot of bitterness for each other, and arguing frequently, the house will be filled with that resonant feeling. Another couple subsequently moving in will find themselves living in a space that encourages this aggressive behaviour. Unless they are well balanced or have an understanding of how to correct such atmospheres, they could well be, during difficult times, drawn into a similar set of experiences. So the energy gets further heightened.

Your House Ch'i

It is interesting to consider why you chose to live in your present house or flat rather than another. Was the choice made for rational reasons, the proximity of a school perhaps, or for its feeling? Perhaps at some deep level of your psyche you have decided to go through a particular set of experiences and the house has provided you with the right atmosphere for that. Many people select a house on its feel. Fortunately, whatever the atmosphere, it is always possible to correct or improve what is there; though this might require specialist help. Whenever I move to a new house, my first task has always been to cleanse and reset the Ch'i.

Feng Shui

In Ancient China the balancing of Ch'i within a house or landscape was known as Feng Shui which literally translated means 'wind' and 'water'. Its origins lie in the Tao, where it was appreciated that the harmonious relationship of objects produced a harmony within the 'Self'. The Feng Shui master would be consulted on the orientation of buildings, and ways to ensure that good

Ch'i flowed through them. Destructive energy known as Sha was to be avoided at all costs. Feng Shui is a fascinating subject and is based upon the eight tri-grams of the I Ching. There are aspects of it that can easily be translated across into a Western society, but some elements cannot so easily be conveyed to a Western mind. For example, Sha was seen to travel in straight lines and therefore alignments of all types had to be very carefully balanced to cause positive Ch'i to flow through them. Much Western architecture has been based on alignments, such as the boulevards of Paris, which would have been abhorrent to the Chinese.

Within a building designed by a Feng Shui consultant, each item of furniture would be carefully placed to ensure this harmonious flow of Ch'i. To assist this, they would use mirrors, chimes and screens to create a harmony.

Many years ago I heard a tale from an assistant to a shipping magnate based in Hong Kong, who had just put up a new office suite. He had been advised to consult a Feng Shui expert, but chose to ignore this suggestion on the basis that it was superstitious nonsense. As soon as the offices were completed his business started to go downhill and it was only in extreme desperation, when he was near to ruin, that he finally relented and brought in the Feng Shui man. Apart from a few minor changes within the building, all that this consultant did was to reorientate the desk of the executive. Within a very short period the business turned around completely, becoming very prosperous. This may, of course, have been a wonderful coincidence excepting that at an anecdotal level many have had similar experiences. Feng Shui is becoming increasingly popular today in Western society.

There is not the scope in this book to go into precise detail of Feng Shui methods, but perhaps its most interesting element is recognising that it is based upon the harmonious relationship of eight archetypal energies. In Western terms these eight principles can be translated into the following headings and room relationships.

- Creativity and Kingship – study
- Transformation and Cleansing – bathroom
- Clarity and Beauty – kitchen
- Joy and Nourishment – dining room
- Wisdom and Growth – living room or bedroom
- Harmony and Love – bedroom
- Peace and Gentleness – living room or bedroom
- Faith and Inner Awareness – hallway

In terms of Feng Shui each room of the house, depending upon it orientation, would have been dedicated to one of these principles and its relationship with the other rooms would be considered carefully as to whether the right Ch'i flowed between them. Later in this chapter we will also look at alternative ways to apply these principles to your homes and places of work and how you can cleanse and set new atmospheres in rooms and buildings.

Hauntings

Another type of related problem occurs where an individual dies but does not realise what has taken place. This can happen in a natural death where the individual cannot accept an idea of an afterlife. More often it happens in cases of murder, suicide or accident. In the latter case the spirit can be ejected from its body in a total state of confusion. The film *Ghost* accurately described this type of experience. These spirits will often become locked into reliving their experiences on earth, making it very hard for those beings on the next plane to reach them. Within a property they can sometimes be aware of others around them, in the same way that those who have a near death experience can see those in the physical world, but cannot communicate with them. This can cause a great deal of frustration and resentment within the departed soul. Whether these eventually manifest as full-blown hauntings with apparitions, or just exist as a 'presence' or 'feeling', is dependent upon a number of other factors.

A number of years ago I visited a house, built around 1880, of a young couple I had got to know locally. They were telling me about a whole series of problems that they had experienced since they moved in. I was suddenly conscious of the presence of a grumpy old man, dressed in clothes from the turn of the century. He seemed most put out that his house had been taken over. Mentioning this to the couple I said that I would release this spirit for them, which I easily and quietly did there and then. The exercise took no more than a few minutes. When I reopened my eyes, the husband had gone as white as a sheet, for although somewhat sceptical, he had felt a sudden intense coldness, as the clearing was carried out. That feeling changed as soon as the spirit had left and the atmosphere had been reset.

One of the more bizarre cases occurred when working with a student on her house. She suddenly became aware of a spirit presence seemingly fast asleep in the corner of the room where a bed could have been. We realised that this soul had died in her sleep (we felt sure it was a woman), with no belief in life after death. She had become trapped in a form of spiritual coma, unable to move on to the next plane. The beliefs or thoughts that we hold at death are very powerful energies as Dr Roger Woolger's research attests. We gently had to awaken this soul and help her on her journey.

All souls that are trapped at this level need help. However some spirits will consciously choose to stay at a place or with a family to protect them. If this is the case it is not appropriate to assist them to move on. Care and discrimination need to be applied. If the spirit appears to be in an aimless or disturbed state then it certainly needs help. The vast majority of all spirits trapped in this way are in a state of relative confusion. They need a great deal of love, help and healing. They should not be condemned to burn in hell, or driven from the place never to return. Sadly I have come across cases of 'exorcism' where the poor spirit has only been driven next door into a neighbour's house. This might be quite funny if you don't get on well with the neighbour, but it does not help the spirit. They must be assisted to make the transition through to the next plane. If this is not done then the 'exorcism' has been a failure. A spiritual connection with the next plane must be made, and the spirit helped to cross that threshold. This is very noticeable when it happens, with an immediate change in the atmosphere and the temperature of the room.

These cases should only be tackled under expert supervision of someone who has had experience of working on this type of case. At no time should they be carried out on your own.

Disturbed Energies

Disturbed energies in places can have many causes. One interesting case involved a friend's house that appeared to have been built over an ancient trackway. A sense of terror and great sadness permeated the length of this path, that on further investigation seemed to have been caused by people fleeing the plague. Apart from my own diagnosis I also independently had the energy lines checked by a dowser colleague. He picked up very similar findings. The fascinating part of this story was that my friend at the time had been suffering a persistent illness that was proving difficult to correct. His homoeopath, about a month previously, had intuitively felt that my friend needed to take a remedy to counteract bubonic plague. This seemed more than a coincidence. In clearing the house we naturally followed the trackway through as far as we were able in both directions.

'Ley' Lines

Another type of energy line in the landscape stems from ley energies. These were first spotted by Alfred Watkins who lived in the early part of the twentieth century. He became aware of lines in the countryside linking ancient monuments. These he wrote about in his book *The Old Straight Track* published in 1925.

There are ley researchers who see these lines only in terms of physical patterns in the landscape, with no suggestion of energy of any description. But from my own working experience they carry many frequencies of energy beyond the physical plane. In some cases lines travelling through an individual's house can upset the people living there. Occasionally these lines are of a chaotic nature, but this is rare. The reason why people get disturbed by them is because they heighten the energies within. It is rather like sunbathing after the winter. If you have not built up a gradual immunity you will get sunburnt. It is not that the sun is bad, just that its energy is too strong to take in, without either plenty of sun cream or a gradual adjustment over several days. These energy lines do not affect everyone in the same way. The more sensitive the individual to subtle forces the more that they are likely to be affected. Helping individuals cope with this type of situation is quite complex and generally requires specialist help.

Energies that are natural to the planet, like underground streams, geopathic stress and strong focuses of Devic energy cannot easily be changed. The best methods involve teaching an individual how to energetically protect themselves from these influences. There are some gadgets on the market today that when connected into the house claim to help. I know some individuals who feel that they have benefited greatly from these devices, but they do not work in every instance. There is also a psychological factor that needs to be taken into account. If someone believes strongly in the efficacy of a treatment then that belief will be a powerful force for improvement.

Healing Treatment of Places

Clearing or balancing any of these types of cases must be approached with a great deal of care. Only those with considerable experience or training should attempt it. The one exception to this rule is any clearings that you do on your own house. Even here, if you suspect any difficult energy is around get others to help you. The hornets' nest in the tree looks harmless enough until it is poked.

The house cleansing exercise given in this chapter involves clearing and resetting an atmosphere within a room, house or building. It does not involve the release of any earth-bound spirits. If you are working on your own house and feel confident that there is no difficult energy around then by all means work on your own. Complete one room first before moving on to the other areas of the house. In all other cases work with at least one other person, where you each have a specific task to fulfil. This type of clearing can either be carried out in the room to be cleansed or it can be tackled from a distance. The vast majority of work that I undertake at this level is done from afar; as in healing people, visiting the place is not necessary.

There are a number of important elements to consider before starting. First, to clear an energy from a room you will need to decide the method you are going to use. Secondly, you must determine what is to be put back in its stead. Remember the saying that 'Nature abhors a vacuum'? Of course, with scientific knowledge today it is easy to produce a vacuum, but at an energetic level, this is an unnatural state. As Christ said it is no good 'casting out a devil, and then leaving the door open for seven more terrible devils to enter'. If you take something out you must put something back.

Energetic Cleansers

The most appropriate cleansers stem from the principles behind the elemental forces of fire and water, which are the two main cleansing agents of nature. In other words you can imagine that you are either washing through a room with water or burning up any disharmonious energy with fire. Some people work with air, visualising strong wind blowing the incumbent energy out of the house into the cosmos. This is fine at one level, but while it removes it from your own space, you can end up dumping it on someone else. This is similar to the way in which the pollutants from Britain get blown into Europe.

The symbol I use most of the time is a flaming sword. In my mind, I will sweep around the whole of the space cleansing all the atmosphere and then send what is left out through the roof into the cosmos. If I chose to work with water, I would imagine a fine shower of rain falling through the room, washing away any impurities and taking the residue deep into the earth to be recycled.

Putting Something Back

Having carried out the clearing work, something now needs to be put back. My recommendation would be to use one of the symbols or colours given in Chapter 6. A good general symbol is a rose, but you could equally use a lotus, caduceus, cross or whatever seems appropriate. You will need to draw on the Ch'i behind the chosen symbol in exactly the same way that you do when giving healing and sense that it is filling the whole of the cleared space. These energies are very tangible. On one occasion, after clearing a property in France, the owner, as well as reporting a considerable improvement in the feeling of the place, said that she was very struck by all the rose water that we must have sprinkled around the place for she could smell it strongly for several days afterwards. The only roses that had been used were those that had been planted at an imagery level in the property. I normally plant the symbol in the middle of the room and imagine its essence filling the whole space, either as a colour or just a feeling.

Healing the energies of places in this way can bring a dramatic change of feeling, particularly if energies have built up over long periods of time. It is as though the house or room has been given a spring clean after years of neglect.

In carrying out this exercise with two people, one person should be solely responsible for protection. They can put a strong protection around themselves, as well as around the person who is doing the clearing. Their partner's task would then be to clear and cleanse the atmosphere, and bring in and set the new energy. If three or more people are involved these tasks can be doubled up, with two carrying out the clearing work and the other person(s) keeping up the protection. When two or more people are working together they should make a special effort to harmonise their energies. They must also be clear about what symbol will be used.

Remember, if you are on your own only work on the rooms of your own house. You could decide from the list given previously which archetypal energies you wish to plant in each room or part of a room if you have a small house or flat. If you have trouble deciding on a symbol here are some that I normally would link to these archetypal principles:

- *Creativity* sun or lion
- *Transformation* winged horse Pegasus
- *Clarity* swan or dolphin
- *Faith* dog or white owl
- *Wisdom* caduceus
- *Joy* rose
- *Harmony* ankh
- *Peace* lotus

You might like to decide for yourself which colours to ascribe to each of these symbols.

The exercise can either be carried out in the room to be cleared or sent at a distance based on two people working together. It can be adapted if you are working alone. It is assumed that you will be carrying out the clearing and your partner putting up the protection.

EXERCISE

Cleansing and Setting Atmospheres in Rooms

(ten minutes)

Aim: *To clear and reset the Ch'i of a room at a mental level.*

- Adopt your normal healing/meditation posture. Close your eyes and attune within, connecting to your inner light. Ask also for help from the cosmos in what you are going to do.
- Feel a strong link and harmonisation of energies between you.
- The protector should now put up a protection both around themselves and around you. They could sense this as a strong spinning bubble of light, imagining that the animal from the

protection exercise is present.

- Now imagine that you have a flaming sword in your hand and sweep it around the room at least three times, cleansing all that is there. Finally see the smoke or residue flowing out through the roof into the cosmos.
- Next, connect to the symbol and feel that you are drawing this down, planting the energy in the room. Sense that the feeling and quality of the symbol is filling every part of the space.
- Finally put a protection around the room, close down your energy and bring yourselves back to full waking consciousness.
- When completed discuss with your partner how you got on and then reverse roles for carrying out the same procedure for another room. With a little practice a whole house can be dealt with in this way in one go.

Summary

- Energies of places can arise from human involvement as well as from natural causes.
- It is quite possible to clear up disturbed energies that people have created. Those that stem from natural forces are much more difficult.
- Disturbed energies, caused by strong emotions within places, can remain for a very long time and are often self-perpetuating, sucking others into similar expressions.
- When spirits die they can sometimes become earth-bound. There can be many reasons why this should happen.

Conclusion

The journey of 1,000 miles
begins with a single step.

(TAO 64)

The proof of the pudding of any system of belief has to be in the eating. Truth is not static, fixed immutably in stone, but has a transient quality, in the sense that as our understanding and knowledge develop so also we can perceive reality from a new perspective. As a channelled source once remarked, 'The only *true* Truth is that moment of realisation when we finally rejoin the Godhead. Everything up to that point is always relative'.

The ideas contained in this book can be used in part or in whole, and applied to many situations outside of the traditionally accepted healing disciplines. It is my hope that they will enrich many aspects of your life as they have certainly done my own.

There is a sense within some mythologies of a 'golden age' when every aspect of life was seen as an expression of harmony with the whole. If we are to survive on this planet we need seriously to address all those issues that cause disharmony, either between ourselves or with the earth as a living planet. As the Tao informs us:

When you know nature as part of yourself.
You will act in harmony.
When you feel one with nature,
You will live in harmony.

(TAO 13)

To find harmony with the earth the first step must be made within, seeking that part of wholeness and balance between all aspects of your being.

Some Organisations Providing Training Courses In Healing

Atlanta Association
33 Beacon Hill Court
Beacon Hill
Hindhead
Surrey GU26 6PU
Tel: 01428 605412

The College of Healing
Runnings Park
Croft Bank
West Malvern
Worcs WR14 4BP
Tel: 01684 565253

The National Federation of Spiritual Healers
Old Manor Farm Studio
Church Street
Sunbury-on-Thames
Middx TW16 6RG
Tel: 01932 783164

British Alliance of Healing Associations
The Seekers Trust
Addington
West Malling
Kent ME19 5BL
Tel: 01372 373241

The White Eagle Lodge
Brewell Lane
Rake, Nr Liss
Hants GU33 7HY
Tel: 01730 893300

Spiritualist Association of Great Britain
33 Belgrave Square
London W1
Tel: 0171-235 3351

Sufi Healing Order of Great Britain
29 Grosvenor Place
London Road
Bath
Avon BA1 6BA
Tel: 01225 312694

Glossary Of Terms

Allah: The Muslim name for God.
Ancestral: That which is derived or inherited from direct ancestors.
Archangels: The highest order of beings from the angelic kingdom. Most notable are Michael, Raphael, Gabriel and Uriel.
Aura: The composite energy fields that surround all life forms.

Bi-location: The ability of consciousness to be in two places at the same time. This is sometimes perceived visually where an individual is seen in two different places at identical times.
Buddha: The founder of Buddhism who lived from 566 BC to 486 BC.

Chakras: Vortices of energy generally along the front of the body that connect the spiritual realm to the physical. There are traditionally said to be seven main chakras.
Ch'i: Subtle energy of the cosmos, that provides form and sustenance to the manifest world. This energy can be manipulated to an extent by conscious thought.

Deva: Literally 'the shining ones' from Sanskrit, referring to a group of spiritual beings who reside over the world of nature. Equivalent to the angelic kingdoms in Christian, Judaic and Islamic belief.
Dis-ease: Dis-harmony or conflict at any level between or within the different elements that link the physical to the spiritual body. This principle applies to all life forms, but in human beings is seen broadly as relating to the physical, emotional, mental and spiritual aspects of our make-up.
Distant healing: The projection of healing energy

(Ch'i) to someone or something not present with the healer.
DNA: Deoxyribonucleic acid; the basic life molecule that contains the genetic code that is found within each cell of a living organism.
Dowsing: A method of obtaining information, using either a pendulum, divining rod or other implement which magnify the subtle sensations of the physical body.
Dualism: The philosophical notion of two distinct principles existing in all things. Similar to the concepts of yin/yang but generally carrying an idea that one is opposed to the other like good and bad or light and dark. Within human beings this is taken to mean that the mind or soul and the physical body are two separate entities often at conflict with each other.

Ego mind: The aspect of the self, aware of its individuality, that has a consciousness of and reflects the different elements of the physical world. Therefore it tends to respond more readily to the needs and appetites of the physical and emotional self as opposed to the spiritual self.
Emotions: The feeling expression of the self, that includes joy, sadness, anger, hate, love etc.
Energy: A force that has an ability or capacity to produce an effect on whatever it is directed towards.
Exorcism: The process of removing a 'spirit' presence from a space, such as a house, or from a person.

Feng Shui: Literally 'wind' and 'water'; relates to the Chinese notion of being able to balance the Ch'i or energy of a place, by the right orientation of buildings, rooms, furniture etc.
Four elements: Traditionally recognised, in many cultures, as four principles that weave through all aspects of the formative and manifest world. At a physical level this is seen as relating to earth, air, fire and water. Within human beings this relates to the four principles of sensation, feeling, thinking or intuition or the four humours of sanguine, choleric, phlegmatic or melancholic.

Geopathic stress: The notion of a subtle destructive energy that stems from the earth.
Ghost: The manifestation of an 'earth' bound spirit.
Guides: Spirit beings who assist incarnate individuals.
Guru: A spiritual teacher.

Haunting: A place where the presence of a ghost is perceived or felt.
Healer: One who consciously projects out healing energy or attempts to bring harmony and balance to another.
Healing: The process of adjustment that seeks wholeness or balance. This can either be experienced within the self or projected out towards another.
Higher self: The aspect of the spiritual self that is directly in touch with the spiritual realm as opposed to the soul which is the aspect of the spiritual self that connects through to the mind and body.
Hypnotism: A process of trance induction that by-passes some aspects of the 'Ego mind' to gain access to the deeper layers of the self.

I Ching: Literally the 'Book of Changes', that stems from Ancient China. It is based on the concept that eight primary principles are found in all aspects of life. The combination of these principles gives 64 hexagrams that formed a divinatory oracle that was used to gain insights into the prevailing spiritual forces in operation around the question asked, so helping the querent make the right decision.
Invasions: Chaotic energy or Ch'i that stems from an outside influence that attaches itself to the energy field of an individual.

Jesus Christ: The founder of Christianity believed to have been born c. 4–8 BC and died around AD 33. Accepted by many to be the son of God in the sense of his very close relationship with the Deity.
Jing: Ancestral energy expressed both through sexual release and the genetic coding.
Carl Jung: Swiss psychiatrist who founded the analytical psychology movement. He lived from 1875 to 1961.

Kabbalah: A mystical system of knowledge that stemmed from Judaic belief. It was originally handed down through secret oral instruction from teacher to pupil.
Karma: The Hindu and Buddhist belief based on the law of cause and effect. Principally seen over the span of a number of lives where the results or deeds of one life set the pattern for what happens in the next.
Kwan-Yin: The Chinese goddess of mercy.

Lao Tzu: The legendary founder of Taoism from his book called the *Tao Te Ching*.

Thought to have been born c. 604 BC.
Law of polarities: *See* yin/yang.
Leys: At a physical level these are seen as alignments within the countryside, particularly in Britain, that link together places of antiquity. These include ancient churches, stone circles, burial mounds etc. and often have remnants of straight trackways linking these sites. First proposed by Alfred Watkins who published a book called *The Old Straight Track* in 1925. These alignments and the various focal points on them are thought, by some, to hold energy over a number of spectrums or frequencies that can heighten spiritual awareness or psychic perception.
Lotus posture: A cross-legged posture, where the instep of the foot rests on the opposite thigh, developed as part of Hatha Yoga.

Madonna: the mother of Jesus often worshipped as an intermediary. There have been a number of visionary sightings of the Madonna most notable of which is at Lourdes. In consequence, this has now become a place of pilgrimage and healing.
Mantra: A word that is repeated either audibly or inwardly as part of meditation discipline.
Meditation: A generic word covering a wide range of different mental methods of connecting to the inner source of our being.
Metaphor: An idea or visual image used as a substitute for something else.
Mind: An aspect of the self that is the seat of conscious and sub-conscious awareness. It bridges between the spiritual self and the emotions.
Morphic resonance: A concept postulated by biologist Rupert Sheldrake whereby the memories or habits of nature are communicated within species and across generations. This information is held within a 'morphogenic field' which surrounds and links together all living things.
Mudras: A system of inner development based upon holding the hands in set positions. These poses create a resonant energy that links together different aspects of the self.

Near death experience (NDE): A widely based experience which generally occurs when the physical body seems to die, but can sometimes happen spontaneously. In the experience, part of the consciousness appears to detach itself from the body and is aware of what is taking place from a perspective separate from the body. Sometimes these individuals will then feel that they are travelling through a tunnel into another dimension where they often report meeting others whom they know have already died.

Neuro-linguistic programming (NLP): The art and science of personal excellence founded by John Grinder and Richard Bandler. Based upon a study of three famous therapists it was perceived they used similar underlying patterns in resolving problems. NLP tries to reframe the way that we think about our reality to bring about change.

Noble middle path: A tenet of Buddhism that seeks a balance between extremes.

Past-life therapy: A system of healing that seeks to bring relief to behavioural patterns that stem from a past-life experience.

Personality types: A method of categorising human characteristics under a number of set headings. At its simplest level it classes individuals as either introverted or extroverted.

Possession: A form of invasion (*see* Invasions) where the invasive force is seen as having a distinct personality or is recognised as a separate 'spirit entity'.

Prayer: A verbal plea or request made either outwardly or inwardly asking for help or intercession from a higher being or deity.

Psyche: From the Greek meaning 'breath'. Taken to refer to the human soul or inner motivating life force.

Psychic diagnosis: A way of using the psychic faculty to gain insights and information not apparent from the five physical senses.

Psychic faculty: An innate human skill that allows us to communicate and experience different levels of perception outside of time or space.

Psycho-kinetic: The ability of the mind to influence physical objects, apparatus or machinery causing them to move or change in ways outside of the known laws of physics.

Pythagoras: Greek philosopher and mathematician who was born c. 560 BC. He is principally known for his famous theorem, but he also discovered the link between proportion and musical harmony.

Regression: An induced state either by another or through oneself for accessing below the normal layer of the conscious mind.
Reincarnation: The belief that each soul lives a number of separate and distinct lives.
Resistance: Anything that causes a barrier to the flow of energy.
Resonance: A concept that explains how energy is transferred between things or people on a non-physical level. Based on the notion that when two objects are pitched musically at the same frequency energy is exchanged between them.
Runes: An ancient Norse and Teutonic magical alphabet used for divination and casting spells.

Sephiroth: The archetypal forms, sometimes seen as attributes of God, that form the basis of the Kabbalah.
Shaman: A word that has recently taken on a wide meaning. Originally referred to the 'magician spirit healers' of Finland and Central Asia, it is now applied widely to all individuals who espouse similar beliefs. One of the main magical symbols of the shaman is the drum which is used to summon up spiritual energy or spirit beings.
Shen: The 'spirit' in Taoist and Ancient Chinese belief.
Soul: The aspect of the spirit that directly links into the body.
Spirit: The eternal divine part of the self that contains the sum total of all individual experiences, whether from this life or previous lives.
Spiritual self: Another way of describing the 'spirit' (*see* Spirit).

Tao: 'The Way'; understood in Ancient Chinese and Taoist belief to mean the 'way of right action'. This would be interpreted through the I Ching and was dependent upon prevailing situations of the time. In all cases the individual wold try to ally themselves with the highest human and moral principles.
Tao Te Ching: The book reputed to have been written by Lao Tzu that describes the 'way of right action'.
Tarot: A divinatory system based on 78 cards that are divided into a Major Arcana of 22 cards and a Minor Arcana of 56 cards.
Telepathy: The ability of the mind to communicate directly with another mind across space and time.

Theosophical Society: A metaphysical philosophical society founded by Madam Blavatsky in 1875. It espoused many Eastern concepts such as reincarnation, but is perhaps best known for its doctrine on the Masters, who are claimed to be high initiates looking after the development of the world.

Transactional analysis (TA): A system of psychotherapy founded by Dr Eric Berne in the 1960s that is based on the notion that we move between alternating personality aspects of parent, adult and child. His system sought ways to balance these elements within.

Transcendental meditation (TM): A system of meditation introduced into the west by Maharishi Mahesh Yogi in the 1960s. It is based on the repetition of a mantra or word.

Vesica Pisces: An important geometrical symbol of two interlocking circles of equal size, where the centre of one circle falls on the circumference of the other. This symbol was a cornerstone of sacred geometry and used extensively in Gothic architecture.

Yang/yin: The concept developed in Ancient China that perceived everything within the formative and manifest world being based upon the interplay of two forces, that are both opposite and complementary at the same time. Yang is the outgoing principle, while yin is receptive.

Yoga: The word is derived from the Sanskrit and means 'union'. Generally this is taken to mean 'union with the spiritual self'. There are many different schools of Yoga of which the best known in the West is Hatha Yoga which works with different body postures to attain higher states of consciousness.

Yogi: The term for an Indian holy man who follows one of the traditional systems of yoga.

Bibliography And Recommended Reading List

Foreword and Introduction

Healing Words, Larry Dossey (HarperCollins, 1993)
Healing Research, Daniel Benor (Helix Verlag, 1993)

Chapter 1

Ch'i Kung, James MacRitchie (Element, 1993)
Margins of Reality: The Role of Consciousness in the Physical World; Robert Jahn & B. Dunne (Harcourt Brace Jovanovich, 1987)
Tao Te Ching, Translated by Gia-Fu Feng & Jane English (Vantage Books, 1989)
The Eagle's Quest, Fred Alan Wolf (Thorsons, 1992)
The Tao of Peace, Diane Dreher (Mandala, 1990)

Chapter 2

Twins, Peter Watson (Sphere, 1984)
Life After Life, Raymond Moody (Bantam, 1978)
Return from Death, Margot Grey (Arkana, 1985)
On Death and Dying, Elizabeth Kübler Ross (Tavistock, 1970)
The Tibetan Book of the Dead, Translated by Robert Thurman (Aquarian, 1994)
Other Lives, Other Selves, Roger Woolger (Aquarian, 1994)
Twenty Cases Suggestive of Reincarnation, Ian Stevenson (University Press, Charlottesville, 1974)
Many Lifetimes, Denis Kelsey & Joan Grant (New York, 1967)
Natural Creation of Natural Selection, John Davidson (Element, 1992)

Karma and Reincarnation, Hiroshi Motoyama (Piatkus, 1992)
The Presence of the Past, Rupert Sheldrake (Fontana, 1989)

Chapter 3

How to Meditate, Lawrence LeShan (Thorsons, 1993)
The Silent Path, Michael Eastcott (Rider, 1975)
The Three Minute Meditator, David Harp (Piatkus, 1993)
Increase Your Energy, Louis Proto (Piatkus, 1991)
Meditation in a Changing World, William Bloom (Gothic Image, 1987)
Meditation – A Basic Course (Atlanteans, 1980)

Chapter 4

Psychic Self-Defence, Dion Fortune (Thorsons, 1994)
A Handbook of Psychic Protection, Draja Mickaharic (Rider, 1993)
Practical Techniques of Psychic Self-Defence, Murry Hope (Aquarian, 1993)
Subtle Body, David Tansley (Thames & Hudson, 1977)
Radionics and the Subtle Anatomy of Man, David Tansley (Health Science Press, 1972)

Chapter 5 and Chapter 10

Hands of Light, Barbara Ann Brennan (Bantam, 1988)
Light Emerging, Barbara Ann Brennan (Bantam, 1993)
Your Healing Power, Jack Angelo (Piatkus, 1994)
I Fly Out With Bright Feathers, Allegra Taylor (Fontana, 1987)
Spiritual Healing, Alan Young (DeVorss, 1981)
The Awakened Mind, Max Cade & Nona Coxhead (Wildwood House, 1979)
Joy's Way, Brugh Joy (Tarcher, 1979)
Therapeutic Touch, Dolores Krieger (Prentice Hall, 1979)

Chapter 6

Colour Healing, Mary Anderson (Thorsons, 1975)
The Encyclopaedia of Traditional Symbols, J. C. Cooper (Thames & Hudson, 1978)
Symbolic and Mythological Animals J.C. Cooper (Aquarian, 1992)
Illustrated Encyclopaedia of Myths and Legends, Arthur Cotterell (Cassell, 1989)

Through Music to the Self, Peter Hamel (Element, 1978)
Sound Medicine, Laeh Garfield (Celestial Arts, 1987)

Chapter 7

I Ching, Translated by Richard Wilhelm (Routledge & Kegan Paul, 1968)
The Illustrated I Ching, R. L. Wing (Aquarian, 1982)
Beyond Psychology, Nona Coxhead (Mandala, 1991)
We've Had a Hundred Years of Psychotherapy and the World's Getting Worse, James Hillman & Michael Ventura (Harper, 1992)
The Black Butterfly, Richard Moss (Celestial Arts, 1986)
Inevitable Grace, Piero Ferrucci (Aquarian, 1990)
You Can Fight For Your Life, Lawrence LeShan (Thorsons, 1984)
The Act of Will, Roberto Assagioli (Aquarian, 1994)
Transpersonal Development, Roberto Assagioli (Aquarian, 1993)
Feel the Fear and Do it Anyway, Susan Jeffers (Harcourt Brace Jovanovich, 1987)
Memories, Dreams, Reflections, Carl Jung (Fontana, 1977)
Owning Your Own Shadow, Robert Johnson (Harper, 1991)
The Complete System of Chinese Self-Healing, Stephen Chang (Aquarian, 1989)

Chapter 8

Where Science and Magic Meet, Serena Roney-Dougal (Element, 1991)
Waking Up, Charles Tart (Shambala, 1986)
The Paranormal, Percy Seymour (Arkana, 1992)
The Nature of Things, Lyall Watson (Hodder & Stoughton, 1990)
Living Magically, Gill Edwards (Piatkus, 1991)
Your Psychic Power, Carl Rider (Piatkus, 1988)
The Creation of Health, Norman Shealy & Caroline Myss (Stillpoint, 1988)
Dowsing, Tom Williamson (Robert Hale, 1993)
Medical Palmistry, Eugene Scheimann & Nathaniel Altman (Aquarian Press, 1989)
Chinese Hand Analysis, Shifu Terence Dukes (Aquarian, 1987)
Tarot, The Complete Guide, Cynthia Giles (Robert Hale, 1992)
Olympus – Self Discovery Cards, Murry Hope (Aquarian, 1991)
Russian Fortune Telling Cards, Svetlana Touchkoff (Harper, 1992)

The Book of Runes, Ralph Blum (Guild Publishing, 1985)
An Illustrated Encyclopaedia of Traditional Symbols, J. C. Cooper (Thames & Hudson, 1978)

Chapter 9

The Chakras, Naomi Ozaniec (Element, 1990)
Ray Paths and Chakric Gateways, David Tansley (Daniel, 1985)
The Chakras, C. W. Leadbeater (Quest, 1977)
Kundalini, Ajit Mookerjee (Thames & Hudson, 1982)
Ambika's Guide to Healing and Wholeness (Piatkus, 1993)

Chapter 11

Possessed, Thomas Allen (Doubleday, 1993)
Poltergeists, Alan Gauld and A.D. Cornell (Routledge & Kegan Paul, 1979)
Possession: Demoniacal and Other, T.K. Oesterreich (University Books, New York, 1966)
The Three Pound Universe, Judith Hooper and Dick Teresi (Dell, 1986)
The Boy Who Couldn't Stop Washing, Judith Rapoport (Collins, 1990)
Understanding Obsessions and Compulsions Frank Tallis (Sheldon, 1992)
Living with Schizophrenia, Brenda Lintner (Macdonald & Co, 1989)
Healing the Family Tree, Kenneth McAll (Shadow Press, 1982)

Chapter 12

Electro Pollution, Roger Coghill (Thorsons, 1990)
The Ley Hunter's Companion, Paul Devereux & Ian Thompson (Thames & Hudson, 1979)
The Power of Place, James Swan (Quest Books, 1991)
The Ghost Hunter's Almanac, Peter Underwood (Eric Dobby, 1993)
This Haunted Isle, Peter Underwood (Eric Dobby, 1993)
Feng Shui, Sarah Roosbach (Rider, 1986)
Feng Shui, Derek Walters (Pagoda, 1988)

Index